THE
10 PILLARS
OF WEALTH

THE
10 PILLARS
OF WEALTH

Mind-Sets of the World's Richest People

ALEX BECKER

BROWN BOOKS
PUBLISHING GROUP

The 10 Pillars of Wealth
Mind-Sets of the World's Richest People

Brown Books Publishing Group
16250 Knoll Trail Drive, Suite 205
Dallas, Texas 75248
www.BrownBooks.com
(972) 381-0009
A New Era in Publishing®

1. Business / Self-help / Motivation I. Title

ISBN 978-1-61254-920-0
LCCN 2016937121

Printed in the United States
10 9 8 7 6 5 4 3 2 1

For more information or to contact the author,
please go to www.AlexBecker.org.

 @alexbeckertech   alex becker   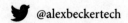 @alexbeckertech

"If your dreams don't scare you, they are too small."

—Richard Branson

CONTENTS

LET'S CLEAR SOMETHING UP

Porn.

I don't know what it is. Maybe most people I interact with have watched too many Hollywood movies. Maybe something about me just screams sleazy. Maybe people just think there is a ton of money in online nudity. Whatever it is, whenever I tell people that I own an online business, they almost immediately assume the same thing:

"He must be one of them fancy-schmancy Internet porn moguls."

Then, after I confirm that no, I do not sell nudie pictures or videos online, they privately assume a whole list of other things such as:

- Credit card scammer . . .
- Stockbroking prodigy . . .
- Hacker . . .
- Mark Zuckerberg genius coder extraordinaire . . .
- Boner-pill seller . . .

. . . and a much longer list of outrageous "jobs" that you would either see in a Hollywood movie or would require lottery-like luck to achieve. Now, it doesn't help my case that one of my good friends is one of the largest porn advertisers online, but assumptions such as that bug the ever-living hell out of me because they're due to people's complete and utter misunderstanding of wealth (and the Internet). That's why I had to write this book: to set the record straight about online businesses and generating wealth in general.

You see, this exact conversation represents the number one reason so many people will never have financial freedom. It represents why less than 1 percent of people ever become millionaires. It represents the primary reason why people choose to work eight-to-five, soul-killing jobs.

If you ignore all the silliness from the first page of this book, you can take away one very ugly, poisonous belief that has been ground into the majority of our heads. One belief that is so damaging that it makes it virtually impossible for you to ever become rich and successful. In fact, the first step to ever becoming successful is recognizing this belief and murdering it with a medieval battle-ax.

"Okay, Alex. Shut up already. What is this belief you're talking about?" It is the idea that, to become rich, something extraordinary, rare, or lucky has to happen. You have to cheat the system, trick people into giving you money, be a super genius with a loophole, be "lucky," or be a sleazebag to become a success. Or, at the very least, become a porn mogul!

This false belief also says that you have to have something special or be someone special and that being wealthy is not in your control. There is simply no ordinary, straightforward way for an average, hardworking person to become a millionaire. It looks so easy for other successful people you admire, but it would be way too difficult or risky for you to become like them. You might as well just sit in your comfortable chair and watch more late night TV because you simply have no chance at becoming great anyway.

Essentially, this belief is that you can't become successful, for whatever reason your brain tells you. Plain and simple.

This belief has killed any chance that 99 percent of people have to be successful before they even think about getting started. If you are not already successful, you are likely suffering from this in some shape or form. You might not even know it, but you are. You probably think being successful is only for the lucky ones, that it is out of your control, or you're simply comfortable in your own life and afraid to take on what you think is a risk. This book is meant to brutally change that.

Don't get me wrong; there is a process to making money and it requires a lot of drive, determination, and hard work. It is hard, but not in the way you think.

You see, many people view money like playing a slot machine in Vegas. It is hard to win, which really means that it is unlikely to win. And it's because of luck or chance, not because of anything you can control. This is not the type of hard I am talking about, though. Making money is hard, much like playing a video game is hard.

Let me explain. First and foremost, as an avid gamer myself, I can tell you that I have seen some of the most worthless people become gods at certain games online. They are bumbling, lazy, worthless people in real life. But, when you give them a controller, they can outdo the overwhelming majority of the human race.

Why? How on earth can lazy slobs accomplish something so challenging? (Yes, video games can be challenging. If you doubt this, log onto any online game and prepare to be shocked by the freakish level of skill required to compete at a higher level. It can take hundreds of hours and strict concentration to reach this level of play.)

It's simple. They believe they can become insanely good. Then, they play (work at) the game over and over again until they are insanely good. Yes, it's difficult to become an expert at the game they are playing. But, whether you're mastering a video game or making money, if you put enough time and effort into what you want, you can and will get good at it . . . even if you are a "loser" who lives in his parents' basement.

Moneymaking is that type of hard. It's not like getting lucky on a slot machine or a lottery ticket. It's not like winning a radio contest. It's not rare or unlikely and it's not about beating the odds. It's not a situation where one person wins, and therefore thousands or millions of other people must lose. It is something that, if you do it over and over, focus with all of your energy, and adopt the mind-set of a winner, you will become good at it . . . just like video games.

That is what reading this book will accomplish. It will fix your head and force you to believe the truth: making money is something that you, yes YOU, can accomplish. More so, this book will remove all the poisonous beliefs from your head that have disabled you from finding financial freedom in the past and replace them with the same beliefs that successful people have. These beliefs are the pillars they live by and the backbones of their success.

You know that thoughts and beliefs drive every aspect of our lives, right? This is not an opinion; this is a fact that is proven every single weekday morning at 8:00 a.m.

Every morning, all over the world, people wake up so early that it's still dark outside. They get in their generic, ugly sedans and drive through traffic that makes them want to gouge their eyes out. They sit down at neutral-colored desks and get told what to do for eight to ten hours a day. They make just enough money to pay their bills, but never enough to get everything they want. Then, they go back through the horrible traffic, watch mindless TV until they fall asleep, and do it all over again the next day . . . unless it's the weekend, in which they finally have some time to do what they love to do.

People sacrifice five days a week so they can enjoy two. They lose time with their families while doing something they would prefer not to do or even despise. They stress over money and time, wishing they had endless amounts of each. Even worse, they accept that they will never be able to change their lives or live out their dreams.

Why on earth would someone do this? What force could be so strong to cause millions of people to live life this way?

The answer is that millions of people share a common belief that this typical eight-to-five life is the best possible option, or even their only option.

Simply put, beliefs are enough to enslave a person and force them to keep their mediocre lives to forgo working towards the lives they truly want (and are capable of having). But beliefs can also keep a successful person successful, even when the "odds are against them."

Imagine this: a broke man gets an idea and works his way to a net worth of over $10 million in less than two years. He felt so proud of himself that he reached his goal and was truly content with his life. Then, six months later, he is electronically robbed and left with only $5,000. (In real life, he'd probably be able to get his money back from the bank or insurance or however that stuff works. But, for this example, just pretend that he only has $5,000, okay? Thanks.)

What do you think he would do? Would he simply join the traffic-fighting masses, give up on his dream, and work an eight-to-five job for the rest of his life? More importantly, do you think he would behave like everyone else?

Hell no! Everything he has seen and done over the past few years proves that he has a much better option. He believes and knows that all he has to do is work his butt off (the correct way) and he can generate wealth (again). Even if he gets a temporary job to pay the bills and put food on the table, that belief will always be in the back of his head, and he will more than likely jump at the first chance he gets to be successful again.

Now imagine if, in an instant, we took the ex-millionaire's beliefs and put them in the head of every single traffic fighter (my term for a person with an eight-to-five job who isn't very happy with their eight-to-five job) in the world. What would happen if every single person suddenly believed they could start a business and generate as much money as they want?

Well, unfortunately, the world would become a giant ball of chaos. Everyone would turn their cars around, skip work, and start making their own businesses. Large businesses around the world would close down, no one would be able to go to

Starbucks for their iced-latte-extra-foam-whatever, and there would be a workforce epidemic.

Fear not, though, because that will never ever happen. It's just a fact of human nature. There is no possible way for every single human to become self-aware, quit their jobs, and turn into multimillionaires. Beyond that, obtaining these millionaire beliefs, putting them in the forefront of your brain, and actually using them to create wealth and success are also incredibly rare. In fact, it usually (not always, but usually) takes a comic-book-style freak accident to force a person into a situation where they can learn and implement these ideas.

Three of the most successful people I know personally have been bankrupt and homeless at one point. One is worth close to $600 million now, and the other two generate millions of dollars a month in personal income.

How did it happen for them? Well, at one point, their situations got so bad and they were in so much pain that they *had* to find another option. This is quite the opposite of the traffic fighters whose situations stink but are not "that bad." The traffic fighters might complain about their jobs and wish they had more disposable income, but the majority of them do not experience strong mental, physical, or emotional pain. It's this immense pain that causes a change. So, since they don't have it, and they are comfortable (I don't mean happy, I mean comfortable and not feeling forced to do something different) where they are, it's much less likely for them to make a change.

Some people are just born with the desire to be an entrepreneur. I am sure you've seen the fourteen-year-old millionaires on TV and in magazines. Unfortunately, I am not one of those people, and unless you are a fourteen-year-old millionaire and you are reading this book to help you fall asleep or something, neither are you. For the rest of us, it takes a giant shock in our system for us to break our limiting beliefs that impede our wealth.

Unless we are hit with true desperation, pain, anger, fear, sickness, or some other extreme circumstance, we will usually stay in our comfort zone until the day we die. That is why people stay in situations they aren't happy with and why middle class people generally stay in the middle class, but why you also see rags-to-riches stories quite often nowadays.

Imagine you were in the desert and had an oasis that gave you just enough water to survive but never enough to be completely fulfilled. Sure, your oasis sucks a big bag of rocks, but you would likely never leave to look for another oasis if it meant risking your small-yet-shitty, comfortable oasis. In fact, the only thing that could ever push you to find something better was your oasis drying up or an invasion of poisonous snakes or something equally as terrifying or detrimental to your health. It's a sad thought, but the only way most people achieve true motivation to improve their lives (in a massive way) is when their oasis has dried up and they are in such a bad spot that they have to make a change.

This is actually how I reached my success. My oasis had dried up and I no longer had the option of staying comfortable.

At twenty-three years old, I was just out of the Air Force and I had nothing. Nothing.

By the time I was twenty-four, I was generating multiple five figures a month in income.

By the time I was twenty-five, I had a business net worth of multiple millions and bought my first Lamborghini.

By the time I was twenty-six, I was generating multiple millions a year. I had moved into my dream house in Uptown Dallas and ran a business that affected thousands of people.

And now, at twenty-seven, I am on the cusp of selling one of my companies for upwards of $20 million, and I am generating hundreds of thousands each month while truly living my life exactly how I want to live it.

Confused? Surprised? Jealous?

Let me explain.

When I was twenty-two years old, I was nearing the end of my four-year term with the American Air Force. The military was good for me. I personally hope my future children join as well, because they sure as hell won't be living off of my money after they turn eighteen. The Air Force made me grow up quickly and taught me how to take care of myself like an adult.

However, while the military was great, my job in the military was not. I do not fault it for a second, though, because it gave me the greatest gift I have ever received. That gift was that it royally pissed me off, which made me desperate to change my life.

I worked in a place where our managers were not military, but promotion-driven civilians. In the military, you cannot quit your job, and you cannot complain about it to your bosses. Because of these facts, the promotion-driven civilians worked us to the bone to make themselves look better.

I was an Aircraft Firefighter during my four years in the service. On most bases, an Aircraft Firefighter would spend his time training and fighting fires as the title entails. However, 99.9 percent of my time was spent cleaning and washing fire trucks. I learned more about cleaning toilets and mopping floors than I did about fighting fires. I remember one month where we had to clean the trucks every single time they left the station because our fool of a boss was terrified that our upper management would be mad if they were dirty.

Note: trucks left the station about ten times a day, including in the middle of the night. Also note that it takes anywhere from forty-five minutes to one hour to clean one fire truck from top to bottom.

Long story short, after cleaning my fifteen-hundredth (or so) toilet, I had had enough. I wanted to move on after my term was up and do something new. There was just one tiny little problem: I had no real-world skills. The firefighter training that was provided in the Air Force was very specialized and did not carry over too well in the super competitive career field of firefighting. And I didn't want to make a living cleaning toilets for the rest of my life.

So, I had two choices: extend my time in the military and endure another four years of doing something I absolutely hated with all my heart and soul *or* do something mildly absurd and try to learn how to make enough money to live off of when I got out of the military.

Being a stubborn moron, I went with option B. Sure, I could have gone to college, but it would have meant scraping by for another four years while all my friends surpassed me. And today, instead of writing a book while having millions of dollars in the bank, I would be taking final exams and wondering what I wanted to be when I grew up. And sure, I could have gotten an entry-level job after I left the military, but as you can tell by now, I am not the type of person who would ever be okay with working for ten dollars an hour to help my boss make six or seven figures a year.

So yes, I chose to do something crazy and figure out how to make money all on my own. I went to my computer and started digging around dozens of forums and websites to learn ways to generate an income online. I ended up stumbling upon a method called SEO.

Now, before I get into what SEO is, I need to reinforce one point. This book is not here to encourage you to learn SEO or to teach you SEO. In fact, the way I made my millions has very little to do with SEO. I am also not endorsing any one particular method of generating wealth. There are 1,001 ways (or more) to do it, but they can all be obtained by following the ideas in this book.

With that being said, SEO (Search Engine Optimization) is the process of improving the ranking of a website on search engines such as Google. All companies want this. Imagine that you own a home security system company. If your company showed up in the top five search results for the search term "home security systems" on Google, this would drastically increase your sales because your company and website would be more visible to your target audience—people searching for

9

"home security systems." How does it end up in the top five search results? By having someone do SEO for you.

The most common ways to make money with SEO do not involve owning the business, though. More often than not, people make money by giving high rankings and promoting other people's products for a commission. They will also do freelance SEO work for outside businesses to increase the amount of traffic the business's site receives. Since you do not have to create anything, this makes the entry barrier remarkably small.

There is much more to it, but this is all you need to understand about SEO right now. If you are interested in learning more, just Google "Source Wave," and you will find my SEO business where we create SEO software and services, as well as train people to do SEO.

Once I discovered SEO, that meant that I found a way to leave the Air Force and still generate a decent income with virtually no education. All I had to do was learn SEO well enough to rank websites and learn how to sell my services to businesses. Then I could get out of this hell hole, move to a college town with my friends, and spend my time getting drunk while making "Internet money." A.k.a.: quit my stable job that I hated and try to make money online.

Unless you're an entrepreneur yourself, this probably sounds like a pretty stupid idea. In fact, this probably makes me sound quite similar to those people who buy "get rich quick" late-night infomercial products. But my job was so awful and my future was so undecided that I decided to choose the "stupid" path and hope that it worked out in my favor.

Unfortunately, I was terrible at SEO. I had never developed the learning skills to improve quickly at something. In the American school system, we are taught to memorize equations and definitions and to color inside the lines. We are never taught how to learn a random skill and become proficient at it. This is a big reason why so many people fail at starting a business. They are not stupid, they just don't know how to learn. We will be fixing that in this book.

Back on subject, my re-enlistment date came up and I had yet to truly make any substantial money. I had successfully ranked a few websites and was able to make some money doing freelance work online, but I had yet to come close to actually replacing my income.

Even though I wasn't making much money with SEO, I still decided that leaving the military and working on my business was the right decision for me. I couldn't stay at a job I hated just to have a steady paycheck. So, I took the final $6,000 from my retirement account and left the Air Force. This put me in a real make-or-break situation. I either had to learn how to generate a substantial income within six months or go broke. This make-or-break situation forced me to take major action to survive.

See, people rarely become successful if they are comfortable in their current situation, no matter how good or bad it is. However, if someone is in physical, mental, or emotional pain from their situation, they are much more likely to take action, take risks, and work towards seemingly crazy goals. It is this pain that drives people to succeed.

This is why smokers can easily quit smoking when they get diagnosed with lung cancer. This is why people easily take medicine when they are sick but always forget to take their vitamins to prevent illnesses in the first place. And this is why I was able to make money with SEO after I realized I had no other option that would have made me happy and successful.

This is one of the reasons why I believe many people get rich. They get so freaking sick of their life situations that they *have* to go against what has been ground into their heads their entire lives. They cannot bear continuing life the way it is. Then, once they find out how to make money, they can't bear not making more.

Like I stated before, the richest people I know personally with net worths ranging from $50 to $600 million have all been bankrupt or homeless at one point. Extremes such as this compels us to ignore everything that we have been told our entire lives and forces us to take drastic action to escape.

Now let's get back to my story. Once I was out of the Air Force with my last $6,000 and no formal education, I was confronted with immense pain. I could not bear the thought of being seen as a failure by my friends and family. My entire life, I was known to be a "fudge up." I couldn't hold a job before the military, and once I finished four years in the Air Force, I wasn't qualified to do anything more than clean toilets. Unless I did something drastic, my future would hold nothing but embarrassment and a life of just scraping by cleaning bathrooms. After experiencing the latter for four years in the Air Force, I couldn't go back. I could not accept the consequences of not changing my life. I valued my life and my pride too much to fail, and once this reality hit me, I suddenly became Superman. I started working for sixteen hours straight with ease, and every thought that crowded my brain was about becoming an SEO expert.

Because of this, I got good at it. Really good. In just a few months, I mastered SEO and Internet skills that take most people years to learn. I made products, I launched sites, and I made cold calls to businesses, trying to get clients. I did it all.

This was not because I was talented. This was because I had the drive to work sixteen hours a day learning and mastering this trade. Anyone can become an expert at anything—even making money—when they put a tremendous amount of thought and time into it. The truth is, most people won't and can't because they don't have the motivation, and motivation is the key. Motivation, however, is near impossible to trigger without an extreme situation. (Have I dug this idea into your brains yet?)

With that being said, I got good enough at SEO that I was generating a decent full-time income. More importantly, I gained the belief that I could make money as long as I worked really, really hard at it.

Because of the skills I picked up, I was offered a full-time job at a marketing agency shortly after I left the military. I was not eager to work for someone else, but this did offer me the convenience of a safety net and comfort zone again, so I took it. To this day I do not regret it, but this is a perfect example of how easily we will cave into something we don't want to do as long as it provides us with a comfort zone.

Regardless, this was a great job with friendly people, and at the time it was my dream situation. On top of that, I was making upwards of $10,000 a month with this job and my SEO freelancing combined. This was more than any of my friends who had college degrees. Because of this, I coasted for a while and was pretty content with my life.

However, the belief that I could make more money if I worked hard at my business lingered in my head. All the success I had up to that point proved it. So, when I desired more money, I could not simply let myself believe that staying in my comfort zone was the right thing to do. I knew that staying in my comfort zone and not changing my daily actions would result in my income also not changing. Because of this, I soon started to resent the long, traffic-filled drive to work. Actually, I despised it. I will not cuss much in this book, but I fucking *hate* rush-hour traffic. Hence my use of the term "traffic fighters" to refer to people stuck in jobs and lifestyles that they hate.

(Disclaimer: a traffic fighter isn't simply someone who has an eight-to-five job. That term is used to describe people who have eight-to-five jobs, *hate* their eight-to-five jobs, and wish they could be doing anything else but that eight-to-five job. But that might not be you or anyone you know. Some people like their jobs and like what they do. Some people are happy with their eight-to-five job and the money they make. However, if you fall into that category, you are more likely to be reading half-baked fiction from a bestseller list than this book. If you are one of these people, more power to you! This book could still help you become more successful at whatever you do. However, this book is truly for people who are *not* happy with their jobs or with the amount of money they make, because these are the people who are much more likely to change and become giant successes.)

After a while, I realized that I hated how my boss ran this agency. I hated having to work five days a week just to "earn" two off. I hated getting paid $10,000 per month when I knew that my boss was making ten times more. This was all because of that belief that had been embedded in my head when I was just working for myself. Yes, this was my dream job, but I was angry all the time because I knew I could make more money on my own. This is a perfect example of how powerful beliefs are.

With that being said, I began to work on my own business every second I got so I could grow it enough that I could quit my marketing agency job. When I got home from my job, I worked. While my friends were playing video games at night, I worked. While everyone I knew was at the pool drinking on the weekend, I worked.

Then, two months later, I was generating over $20,000 a month from my business, not including my job's paycheck. At that point, I quit my job and never looked back. My boss was a good person and the marketing agency was great, but working for myself prior to having this job had already filled me with the belief that I could control my income. Because of this, I would never be able to work at any office job ever again for any length of time. Even to this day, if I were to lose everything, I would get a job to pay my bills and buy some food, and then, almost immediately, I would start working on creating a new business. Why? Because I know I can be successful working for myself.

Because of the pain I had in my life, I was inspired to take massive action. In fact, taking that amount of action was pretty easy because I saw no other option. Because of the action, I gained beliefs that pushed me again to go further. And, because I kept pushing myself to go further, I learned how to control my money and income. The farther down the rabbit hole I went, the more I learned the mind-sets and beliefs needed to generate millions of dollars in income. I learned the core beliefs (or what I like to call pillars) that all successful people have and all unsuccessful people lack.

What I want to do with this book, though, is give you the shortcut to the final step: controlling wealth and income. I would love for you to skip the "massive pain" step that many of us encounter and simply gain the mind-set to have more control over your life. More so, I want to give you the exact pillars that have made me and many others extremely wealthy.

Obtaining this knowledge usually takes extreme pain and slow belief building. But, if you're reading this book, you have probably not gone through a situation where the need to succeed was stronger than the need to stay comfortable. Not yet, at least.

Don't get me wrong, I was not in a serious situation and I am not some rags-to-riches story. All the mental pain I felt was self-inflicted, but that still counts! It all simply comes down to that moment when your brain hits a point where it can't take it anymore . . . where something must change or else you'll go crazy. It's different for everyone. It might take a horrible job, going bankrupt, true financial hardship, family traumas, or even being homeless (like my successful friends I mentioned) to make your brain switch from "I can live like this" to "something must change immediately."

However, most people will never reach that point. Why? Because since the day we are born, our society makes us think that mild daily pain is normal and expected and that we can't be content with every aspect of our lives. We also live in a society that loves comfort. And I mean loves it. We are told to go to school, get good grades, get a job, and do well at that job, all so we can make enough money to be comfortable. And even if you dislike your job, you're probably comfortable enough at it that you think changing it is pointless, silly, impossible, or too risky.

People might not like what they do. They may be unhappy or want to be wealthier than they already are. But what they have now is bearable and a far better alternative to taking what they believe to be risks. Because of this, very few people are ever pushed to leave their comfort zones and change their lives. But the fact is that you will not become successful if your life stays the same. You can't expect your life or circumstances or situations to change if you don't change.

That might be why you're reading this book. You don't really like the situation you're in and you think that you might want to change it, and you can safely read this book about becoming rich without taking any risks.

In fact, if you are not already creating a successful business or changing your life in some drastic way, then you are most likely reading this book because you want some way to become wealthy without taking a single risk. Everyone does, and that's part of the problem of which I am going to cure you. In fact, taking risks is one of the core beliefs you need to adopt.

Let me tell you right now: to become rich, you will have to take risks. Let me repeat that in another way. You must take risks to be successful. (These must be smart and thought-out risks, but we'll get to that a little later.) Haven't you ever heard of "high risk, high reward"? That also equates to low risk, low reward, which is probably the world you're living in right now.

Over the past few years, my sole focus has been to make money, and then to make more and more of it. I have spent substantial time learning from other multimillionaires personally as well as studying others from afar. And, while the majority of multimillionaires have become successful after a massive hardship, I am going to teach you a way to become wealthy without one. (PS: I mean jet-owner wealthy, not attorney or doctor wealthy. And when I say "successful," I mean owning-apartments-in-three-major-cities successful, not owning-two-Acuras successful.)

Long story short, no matter who you are or what you are doing with your life right now, I am going to teach you the core beliefs and thought processes that will make it impossible for you not to become rich. Better yet, I am giving you these lessons while allowing you to skip the pain that is normally required to learn them. This book will simply allow you to adopt successful people's beliefs. It will give you the push to chase your dreams and the know-how to do so with confidence. If you have been staring at the door of wealth wondering how to get in, this book will give you the key . . . *if* you follow and truly believe everything I write. If you read this book and say, "Cool, that seemed to work for him, but . . . I'm in such a different spot than he was," or, "I'm not sure that'll work for me . . ." then no, this book and these beliefs will not work for you. So, once again, I am handing you the key to success. But you are the one who has to unlock the door.

I have seen every single type of success story possible. I have personally seen a once-homeless person make over $50 million in a single year. I have seen a man, whose first ten businesses went bankrupt, reach a net worth of more than $500 million. I have seen former military members become multimillionaires. I have seen rich kids who went to college get fed up with their jobs and become rich in their own right.

I have seen every type of person in almost every single circumstance you can imagine become successful. In fact, most of them are not even that intelligent, and quite a few are borderline bums. However, every single damn one of them shares the same set of beliefs, including me. On top of this, the more they give into these beliefs, the richer they become.

These are beliefs that poor people will never have nor understand. Some poor people will read this book and call me a fool. They will also call you stupid for wanting to think this way, which reinforces why they are poor in the first place. They do not believe that anyone can go out there and become incredibly wealthy. They certainly do not believe the solution can be found in your head, either.

That's okay though, because they will spend the rest of their lives poor (or "comfortable") and unhappy, while you spend the rest of yours working hard (and smart) and reaching and surpassing your goals.

While they are working for years to get that promotion, you will be giving yourself a promotion every week. When they are counting pennies and budgeting, you will be thinking of everything but money because you have plenty. When they are sixty-five years old, they will look back and wish they had gotten out of their comfort zone, and you will look back and be glad you did.

This is how important these beliefs, mind-sets, and under-standings are. They are so powerful that I will refer to them as pillars over the course of this book. Like pillars that support Greek monuments, they support everything that makes a mul-timillionaire a millionaire.

Once you have these pillars in your head, your world will be a different place, and it will never go back to how it was before. You might even wonder how you ever lived without them.

So, without any further ado, let's begin.

THE 1ST PILLAR

REJECTING GETTING RICH SLOW

Fair warning: If you are new to the idea that you can make as much money as you want and live a life of true freedom, then I'm probably going to piss you off a bit. This is because everything that everyone has ever taught you about becoming successful is completely wrong. Yes, WRONG (unless you were taught by a self-made multimillionaire).

Your dad was wrong.

Your grandparents were wrong.

Your teachers were wrong.

Your friends are probably idiots, and they're also wrong.

People and society are always wrong.

You. Are. Wrong.

Seriously, go for a drive down any highway in any major city around 8:00 a.m. You will see tens of thousands of college-educated people packed bumper-to-bumper, sipping on their shitty convenience store coffees and yelling profanity at the people in front of them. This is undoubtedly not what they want to be doing at 8:00 a.m. five days a week. They're mildly miserable, but they don't think they have any other options, so they live this life every single day until they retire or die.

Does this seem like a group of people who have everything all figured out? Do they seem like the best people to teach you about becoming financially free? While the obvious answer is no, traffic fighters have more than likely been giving you advice on what you should be doing with your life since you were in grade school.

Meanwhile, I decide what I want to do every single morning. Sometimes, I am up at 4:00 a.m. to work and talk to developers. Other times, I wake up around 6:00 a.m. and play four hours of Fallout 4. Then, around 10:00 a.m. when everyone is off the road, I drive my Ferrari to the grocery store to pick up fresh vegetables for my juicer.

Sure, the above paragraph makes me sound like a douche-bag. But guess what? I am doing exactly what I want to do when I want to do it, and I'm having a hell of a time doing it. I love working. I love playing video games and goofing off on my own schedule. I love all sorts of stuff, and I do it whenever I want. And one thing's for sure: you won't find me upset and screaming at strangers on the highway at 8:00 a.m.

Now that you know that both lifestyles are possible and achievable, whose footsteps—the traffic fighters or mine—would you rather follow?

Let's go back to why the traffic fighters' definition of success, and what we are taught our whole lives about the topic, is ass-backwards. We are told to stay on the straight and narrow. "Do well in school, go to college, get a good job, work hard, save most of your money, and retire at sixty-five or seventy. This is the most consistent and low-risk way to reach success and happiness. All you have to do is work hard!"

We are then led to believe that starting a business is super risky, incredibly difficult, and/or similar to playing the lottery. Either you are Mark Cuban or Mark Zuckerberg, or you are not. Either you have a brilliant idea or you are just screwed. (Don't get me wrong, starting a business comes with inherent risks, but these are *good* risks. Good risks are risks that you can control with foresight and proper planning. On the flip side, bad risks are risks that you allow other people to control for you. As you will see in this chapter, sticking to society's path to success is built upon a foundation of bad risks.)

The thought that starting a business "won't work for you" is lethal. It will rob you of your life and leave you as a semi-well-off, old nobody in the best-case scenario. Living this eight-to-five life is actually extremely risky in a bad way. Let me explain why this is the equivalent to an early death from two different perspectives: financial and quality of life.

GETTING RICH SLOWLY

So, let's assume that you had an A average in high school, got into a good college, graduated magna cum laude, and accepted an epic job paying you $70,000 a year. You are also a hard-working badass. So, instead of the average promotion of 3 percent a year, you get 5–7 percent every year. That will equal over $100,000 a year in ten years, and quite a bit more in thirty years. You lucky duck.

THE FINANCIAL RISK AND QUALITY OF LIFE OF GETTING RICH SLOWLY

Is this safe? Is this smart? Let's look at it from a financial point of view.

At this moment, you are sitting pretty fat. In return for giving up five days of your week, every week . . . forever . . . your living expenses will be paid and you will even be able to afford a few cool luxuries every once in a while. You and your family are quite content, especially when you compare your life to your old friends and old relatives who gave you advice when you were younger. You did what they told you to do, and you ended up with a comfortable life. You won't ever be able to get the Lamborghini you always wanted or be a multimillionaire or freely travel the world or have anything that takes an incredible amount of time or money to acquire or experience, but you will do just fine according to most people's standards.

All you have to do is work hard for the next thirty years and then retire. If you save 50 percent of what you make after taxes (let's just assume you average $120,000 a year), you will have $1.8 million in retirement savings. That's not too bad. In thirty years, you can be sort of rich and live off that until you die (as long as you don't spend too much of it).

Sounds like a pretty safe bet. You just have to make sure none of the following events happen:

- You die in the next thirty years.
- You get fired from your job.
- You get laid off.
- Your job gets outsourced.
- Your job becomes obsolete.

And you have to make sure all of the following events happen:

- The company you work for stays successful.
- The economy stays decent.
- The currency your money is saved under stays strong.
- Your investments don't collapse.
- You don't have any major illnesses that stops you from working.

Yep, as long as all those things work out exactly in your favor, you will be a sorta millionaire thirty years from now. (I say sorta millionaire because the true idea of being a millionaire is not ever worrying about money. If you have to save every penny that you earn and then watch every penny once you retire, you are not really living that idea of being a millionaire.)

However, chances are that something negative will happen. In fact, in the twenty-something years I have been alive, all of my family members have been laid off due to the economy, their company going under, etc.

So, if we look at this from purely a financial standpoint, the low-risk-get-rich-slowly or slow-and-steady-wins-the-race mind-set is a borderline lie (or dare I say, a scam) and a recipe for financial ruin.

It is a 100 percent "hope for the best" gamble by all definitions. By nature, a gamble is betting on something for which you cannot personally control the outcome. Every one of the "income killers" that I listed above is 100 percent out of your control, and everything that must stay stable for you to succeed, such as the company for which you work staying profitable, is also out of your control. This is why it is so risky in a bad way. Almost every factor that controls your life is in someone else's hands. Whether it is your boss's, your company's, the economy's, or just freak accidents, your financial well-being is decided by everyone and everything except you, and this is your fault because you are allowing this to happen.

No matter how hard you work, how much money you save, or how educated you become, there is always a chance that the tide will come in and knock over that financial sandcastle that you have been building for thirty years. Even worse, the more time you spend building your retirement nest, the higher the chance that it will get wiped out by one of the setbacks I listed. It's common sense that the longer it takes to build something, the more likely something will go wrong simply due to the amount of time spent building it.

Let me explain. Imagine we are putting a roof on a house, and if it rains, the whole project will be ruined. If we complete the job within twenty-four hours, there is a low chance we will run into rain. However, if it takes us a month to complete the roof, there is a much better chance that at least one rainy day will come and force us to start all over. What people are doing financially is the equivalent to building a financial roof for thirty years and praying it doesn't ever rain.

What you need to understand is that it *will* rain . . . and it will probably rain multiple times throughout your lifetime. So, not only is this get-rich-slowly mind-set horribly risky, it is almost downright impossible in most circumstances. It's getting even worse now with how quickly technology is replacing people in the workforce in combination with the population growth . . . but that's a topic for another time.

Now, as awful as this sounds, I haven't even gotten to the worst part of society's get-rich-slowly mind-set. Instead of focusing on the financial part of this equation, let's focus purely on the quality of life. After all, some people don't care about money and may not want to become filthy rich. You might just want to have a happy, stress-free life.

Let's imagine that everything I just said above is not true. Let's imagine that the world is a perfect place and nothing bad will ever happen to you. You will never get sick or fired, and the company for which you work will stay profitable forever. All you have to do is work hard for thirty years, and then you can retire. This doesn't sound too bad until you remember a few things.

First off, you are going to have to spend all thirty of those years pinching pennies and living a lifestyle focused around saving money. This means your whole life will be limited, so you must live in moderation.

You might want to take your wife to the nicest restaurant in town on a Friday night, but instead you take her to some neighborhood bar and grill because it is "in your budget."

You might want to travel around Europe with your family, but you settle on going to county fair or amusement park for the weekend because it's a fraction of the cost.

You *really* want a Ferrari, but you are forced to drive a pre-owned economy import because owning the car you desire doesn't fit into your thirty-year savings plan.

So sure, you will still be able to get everything that you need and some of the things that you want, but instead of freely giving money away in exchange for luxury items, you will mentally and physically settle for "regular" items, such as fast food and mid-priced cars. But, not only will you be living a moderate life, your focus will be backwards, and your quality of life will go down the toilet. Instead of focusing on doing great things in your present life, you will obsess over saving a buck or two with coupons when you are grocery shopping in the hopes that you have enough money to retire one day—somewhere between twenty and fifty years from now.

Your whole life is spent on limiting yourself now in the hopes of a comfortable future. Don't get me wrong, I am not advocating living outside of your means. However, when you live a get-rich-slowly lifestyle, you are anything but living; you are a slave to money, and you're never actually able to live the life you truly want to live.

In fact, with the get-rich-slowly mind-set, the only time you get to truly sit back and enjoy life is when you are sixty or even seventy years old, and only then *if* you manage to reach that point *and* still be active *and* still want all the things that you wanted when you were younger. This is the big reward at the end of the work tunnel: being old and having enough money to live within your means until the day you die. What type of reward is this?

And don't even get me started on people who say that they will travel (or buy a new car or move to the city of their dreams) once they retire. Wouldn't you much rather travel in your twenties and thirties (and forties and fifties) instead of waiting until you retire, hoping that you and your spouse are both still healthy and agile enough to do so? If you have a desire to do something with your life, do it now. Your future is not promised, and you do not want to be sixty years old wishing that you "lived your life" more at twenty-five instead of saving every penny for a retirement vacation that you never ended up taking.

On top of that, you have just given up 71 percent of your younger life (five days a week is 71 percent of the week, which, in turn, is 71 percent of your life) so that you can "get by" or "sit comfortably" in the latter part of your life. You have given up 71 percent of your life and spent your younger years searching for spare change in the couch cushions, all so you can have some money when you are too old to truly have fun with it.

How is this for quality of life? How is giving up 71 percent of your life, stressing over money, and living a limited lifestyle a positive thing? How does focusing on money instead of love and family and fun equate to having a good life? More so, how is spending your elderly years hoping that you do not run out of money before you die a reward?

In short, my friend, not only is getting rich slowly a high-risk plan for financial ruin, it also substantially lowers your quality of life until the day you die.

This whole chapter is meant to make you realize this and to show you that there is a better way. You don't have to leave your life in the hands of an uncontrollable and unfair system. More importantly, there is a way for you to take your life back from this system and put your fate in your control.

Remember the monetary scenario example I listed above? The one where you reached the age of sixty with around $1.8 million in savings as the best-case scenario, while living a limited life before you retire? After going through everything we just covered, that sounds like a pretty shitty situation, doesn't it?

That's because it is. By age twenty-six, I had already achieved a net worth of eight figures (which means I had far more than $1.8 million in hand). In just two years, I was able to achieve what takes many people their entire lives to achieve. With proper investing, I could easily live off this money until the day I die, while currently having financial freedom and an extremely high quality of life.

You are reading this book because you probably want something similar, but because of what you have been taught your whole life, my achievements seem like a long shot for the average Joe. You also probably believe that doing it my way is financially risky and could possibly lead to a poorer quality of life than the one you currently have.

Our entire lives, we are taught that entrepreneurship (a.k.a. "getting rich quickly") can have substantial rewards. However, we are also taught it is like playing a slot machine in Vegas, and we could end up broke and homeless, so it's simply better to stick with the get-rich-slowly mentality. As I proved above, the get-rich-slowly mentality is not only a true gamble for your present and future but also leads to an overall low or mediocre quality of life . . . average at best.

Let's look at the get-rich-quickly mind-set the same way, from a point of financial risk and quality of life. For you to truly become successful, you have to understand and believe what I am about to explain to you. That is why it is the first pillar in this book.

GETTING RICH QUICKLY

Before I get into anything, I need you to understand one thing. Getting rich quickly is extremely low risk for one and only one reason. YOU CONTROL EVERYTHING. I know this sounds harsh, wrong, or the complete opposite of what you believe, but I'll explain. Just keep reading.

Your mind, what you learn, how hard you work, and every-thing you do directly controls how much money you make. It is a lot like working out or playing a video game. When you start, you are likely going to suck at it, get frustrated, and possibly even quit. This is why people consider it too hard and too risky. Well, it's not. It just has a steep learning curve, and you are likely to fail at first.

However, just as with a video game, if you stick to it, you will eventually get good at it. In fact, if you stick to anything for a year or two, you will get good at it. Guitar, video games, coding, whatever it may be, you will eventually reach a level of competence if you stick with it long enough, put all your energy and focus into it, and have the right tools to master it.

Keep in mind, this isn't like playing a sport where only the .01 percent of players are good enough to make substantial money. Often in business, merely being competent is enough to earn a substantial income. This is off topic, but you will hear false facts such as "only 1 percent of businesses succeed." The truth is that most businesses are built and planned out by people who don't think or plan correctly, and most people give up within a few months because it became too hard or too confusing. With the pillars in this book, you are going to have a huge advantage over these people as you learn how to start a business that works with very little "bad" risk.

Now the good news with getting rich quickly is that you only have to get it right once. You can fail ten times, get your eleventh attempt right, and then go on to be rich for the rest of your life *if* you are smart about it. In fact, even if it takes you fifteen years to finally get it right, you are still in a *much* better spot than the get-rich-slowly person who has to build things up over thirty years, save lots of money, and hope that an unpreventable disaster doesn't happen.

So, the three key ideas to take away from this are:

1. You control your life.
2. You can get better at anything.
3. You are allowed to fail.

So, let's imagine that a person just turned twenty-one. She gets a thirty-hour-a-week job at Costco to pay the bills and/or finds a low-cost way to live. By the way, with proper money management, it is extremely easy to live on less than $1,000 a month (when you are young and single before you rack up lots of debt, at least). For about $600 a month, I was able to fully cover my rent, food, and everything else I needed when I was in this period of building my business. But let's get back to the story.

Now, for two years, this person tries to build a low-investment, high-return business (which I will explain later in this book) in about forty hours a week. That means she works about seventy hours a week total, which is totally doable and quite necessary when building a business.

More importantly, in this situation, her effort and hard work are big factors in her becoming rich; those traits are 100 percent under her control.

Over these two years, she fails over and over again. However, her means of living are extremely low, so nothing really terrible happens when she fails. She simply tries again a different way. On top of this, every time she fails, she learns something else that doesn't work, and she becomes much better every time she tries.

So, like I stated above, nothing bad happens when she fails because of how she has set up her life, *and* she is getting better at what she is doing. By getting better, she will eventually hit some form of success. It is truly just a matter of time. (Just a reminder: You know those people who try and try and never become successful? That is because they give up and quit. It is also because they lack the pillars, which I will show you in this book. It might take you ten years, but if you never give up, you will have something to show for it.)

After these two years, because she has worked very hard and gotten significantly better, her sixth business attempt succeeds. She starts generating $5,000 a month and is able to quit her job to focus on her business full time.

She is now putting in sixty hours a week solely on her business. Then, she replicates what she's doing, expands it, and improves it. Within two more years, her business is making more than $80,000 a month. She is now a millionaire, and with proper investing, she can live off this money for the rest of her life. All in four years of hard work.

I have seen people do this whole process within six months. I have also seen hundreds of people personally go from nothing to millionaire in two years' time. So, as farfetched as this might seem to you, it is possible, and surprisingly not as rare as you may think. If you ever attend one of my events or follow me online, you will see hundreds of people who do this. See some of these examples at AlexBecker.org.

Now, let's take a step back and look at this from a financial-risk standpoint.

THE FINANCIAL RISK AND QUALITY OF LIFE OF GETTING RICH QUICKLY

What were her risks to reach this level of success? Virtually nothing. All she had to do was keep her means of living low. She could fail multiple times because she was starting low-investment, high-return businesses.

(I will get into low investment, high ROI [return on investment] businesses later on, but some examples of these types of businesses are coding, design, and marketing services. All of these businesses only require you to learn and provide a skill. There is very little personal investment required to provide these services. I hope you can accept that it is not only possible but also easy to create this without any major investment. It can even be free in many cases.)

Because of this, while her chances of failure were high when she first began, failing did not mean she would be homeless or owe lots of money from a loan. And, since she wasn't dealing with giant risks, she was able to calmly get better at her business, and her chances for success grew and became inevitable. Once she hit success, she was rich in a drastically shorter time than the get-rich-slowly person, and without the same amount of actual risk.

Do you see how her short-term chances of failing were greater, but the overall risk was low the entire time? Do you also see how her income and financial future were solely controlled by her actions instead of the uncontrollable circumstances that the get-rich-slowly crowd suffers from? This is again a perfect example of a good risk that we can control versus a bad risk that is left to a roll of the world's dice.

Getting rich quickly can be extremely low risk, financially speaking, if you plan the right way. Also, while you might live financially limited for a few years, you will eventually hit a point of complete financial freedom, which is much more appealing than living financially limited for the majority of your adult life while getting rich slowly. This is also why getting rich quickly is easy for someone to transition to at any age. Starting certain online businesses can be low cost and nearly risk free. The only real challenge is having to reduce your lifestyle while waiting to hit success, which, once again, is only for a limited time.

This leads us to the next part—analyzing the quality of life. This is where the true disadvantages of getting rich slowly come into play. As I mentioned before, getting rich slowly requires you to spend 71 percent of your days for the rest of your young life at work. Regardless of your views on money, your time is the greatest sacrifice in the getting-rich-slowly plan. Between the ages of twenty and sixty is the time when you most likely want to travel the world, raise your kids, spend time with your family, chase your dreams, and get the most out of life. The cold, hard truth is that by the time you have finally saved enough money to retire, most—if not all—of those things will have already passed you by. Even worse, there is a good chance you will not be able to retire at sixty due to all the economic downfalls I listed above. Heck, you might not even *live* past sixty, or you might die a week after you retire. Why push off all the fun stuff to an age you might not even reach when you can do it now or in the immediate future?

To me, losing 71 percent of the best years of my life is a horrifying thing to think about. Worst of all, giving up this time has no guaranteed golden reward at the end of the tunnel. You never escape having to live within your means. Your whole life is just one long sequence of worrying about bills and pinching pennies. You are forced to live a life of restriction in three separate areas. These are (from least important to most) luxuries, stress, and choices.

First and foremost, when you play the get-rich-slowly game, you are instantly forfeiting material luxuries. You are giving up buying your dream car, traveling the world, eating at expensive restaurants without stress, and living the life of luxury that most people dream of. I don't know about you, but I want to go through life seeing and doing (and owning) all the amazing things it has to offer. It might not be buying a Ferrari or owning an island, but there is something you want and dream about that is expensive. Maybe you want to be able to send all four of your kids to expensive colleges, pay off your parents' house, or pay the medical bills for your sick cousin. Well, if you play the get-rich-slowly game, your dreams will stay just dreams, and your wildest luxuries will never become reality. Sure, you might be able to buy a nice car and live debt free, but if you desire something every day that never ends up happening, how is that a decent quality of life?

Second, and far more important, is your overall level of stress. When you are living in the get-rich-slowly mode, you are guaranteed to have some form of stress due to money. Why? Because your life is built on living within the limits of your money. Bills, dinners out, and other everyday expenses cause you stress because you only have so much money to work with.

Money can buy just about anything, but the most important thing it can buy is freedom from financial stress. To this day, my lifestyle costs only a fortieth of my monthly income, and every month I put away enough money to last me for years. I have cool toys and go on fun adventures, but more importantly, I have zero financial stress in my life.

When I go out to dinner, I order whatever I want. When my bills come, I barely notice and definitely don't worry about them. And, more importantly, when I wake up, I am focused on life and not its minor (or major) expenses. As long as I am intelligent with my money, I have the ability to go through life never having to worry about it.

On the contrary, when you look at people who are getting rich slowly, they have anything but this. You will see them closely calculating tips at dinner, getting mad over a $25 overcharge on their phone bill, and living off credit and stressing over their credit score. Turning down your air conditioning a few degrees or leaving a light on all day by accident should not be emotional experiences. I haven't looked at my electric bill in months, and I don't plan on it because it does not matter and has no impact on my emotional well-being. Living in stress due to money drastically cuts down your quality of life no matter who you are.

Most important of all, though, are choices and personal freedom. As of right now, I have a lot of choices. I could write this book or I could not. I could wake up tomorrow and work all day or I could play video games all day. I could be on a plane to Spain in the next hour or I can sit in my house for a month without leaving. Heck, I could turn my phone off and ignore the entire world for weeks if I wanted to.

Why? Because I have financial freedom, which allows me to make choices about how I live my life. I can *choose* what I want to do and when I want to do it.

When you play the get-rich-slowly game, your choices are instantly limited. You take vacations when you are allowed to. You have to wake up at a certain time to go to work and do your job. You can't just randomly take a week off and go on a road trip with your wife and kids. You do not control your choices; your boss and your job and your responsibilities control your choices.

Worst of all is that you have to make your decisions *solely* around money.

Right now, I am working on a YouTube channel that is growing. I don't do it for the money; I choose to do it because it makes me happy. Working on my business makes me happy as well. When I get done with those things, I can spend my time with my girlfriend or watch hockey for hours. Money is not the sole factor in my daily, weekly, or yearly decision-making.

In my opinion, having a high quality of life is about being happy and content with your thoughts and actions. When your decisions have to be focused around money, you rarely get to choose what makes you happy. Therefore, your quality of life plummets.

With that being said, let's sum up this chapter.

When you live life in a get-rich-slowly fashion, you:

- Are extremely likely to be put in financial hardship.
- Give up control of your financial future (a.k.a. risks you cannot control).
- Let 71 percent of your young life be monopolized by work.
- Lose any chance of obtaining your dream life.
- Live your entire life under financial stress.
- Can't make your own choices because they are solely based around money and time.

All for the grand reward of being able to scrape by (or hopefully live comfortably) when you are too old to do what you want in life.

On the other hand, when you live life in get-rich-quickly mode, you:

- Control your financial future (the opposite of bad risk).
- Spend your time doing what you want.
- Have a real chance of getting all (or at least most) of the luxuries you want.
- Have a chance to escape financial stress.
- Can make your own choices because they are based around what makes you happy.

This is the idea that you *must* take away from this chapter: At the core of every successful person is an absolute and utter disgust for getting rich slowly. Self-made rich people understand that the lowest-risk bet is to bet on themselves because they control the outcome.

Until you truly take in the ideas that I have listed in this chapter, it will be unnecessarily difficult to reach the level of success you desire. The reason why you hear about so many entrepreneurs going through times of extreme poverty (working out of a garage, sleeping on a dorm room floor, going bankrupt multiple times) is because they understand this concept. Being poor is only temporary when you control the outcome. These entrepreneurs are giving up a few years of semi-comfortable living while working on their businesses in order to spend the rest of their years in getting-rich-quickly paradise.

Entrepreneurs understand that the more you work at something (including making money), the better you will get. Failing a few times is common, but if you learn from these failures and figure out why those attempts didn't succeed, you will eventually hit your target. And the good news is you only need to hit your target once to be rich for life.

This is the first pillar of wealth. Without it, nothing else matters. Until you utterly reject the idea of getting rich slowly and commit to the idea of getting rich quickly, you will never have the drive needed to make your dreams become reality.

Stocks
Personal training
Athletic clothing
Digital marketing

THE 2ND PILLAR
SEPARATING TIME FROM MONEY

I'm sure you have heard the phrase "time is money," right?

You have also probably heard of (or seen) the movie *The Wolf of Wall Street*, yeah? Well, if you haven't, let me fill you in.

The movie is about a famous Wall Street tycoon in the '90s named Jordan Belfort who scammed people out of hundreds of millions of dollars. By the age of twenty-six or twenty-seven, he was making over $50 million a year. With inflation rates, that would be over $100 million a year in 2015. Long story short, Jordan knew how to generate money and generate it fast.

Now, if you saw this movie, you'd remember that almost 90 percent of Jordan's time was spent doing hard drugs, partying, and having sex with prostitutes. In fact, Jordan was routinely so high that he didn't even know what planet he was on.

What I want you to learn from this example is that Jordan spent 90 percent of his time partying his ass off, yet he was still making the equivalent of $100 million a year (in profit!). Does the saying "time is money" apply to this? Nope. This is because time is not always money. If that saying were completely true, Jordan would have become indigent after six months, or never would have become wealthy in the first place.

In the movie, Jordan's immense fortune did not come from his investment of time. It came from his army of stockbrokers and sales floor filled with hundreds of people. When Jordan was passed-out drunk in Vegas, his people were making millions for him. When Jordan was sinking a $25 million yacht, his people were making millions for him. When Jordan was doing *anything*, good or bad, his people were making millions for him.

So how did he do all of this? Jordan essentially created an absolutely lethal sales pitch for cheap penny stocks. Next, he cloned himself hundreds of times by having his stockbrokers memorize this pitch. Then, they were able to push this pitch thousands of times a day to wealthy people on their call lists.

At this point, Jordan's time no longer played any part whatsoever in the equation of wealth. He set up a system (more like a machine) that ran and generated wealth no matter what he was doing with his own time.

In fact, at this point the only factor that controlled his wealth was how well he directed the machine and the business decisions he made. One single decision generated millions of dollars because his machine carried it out. This point is truly nailed home, because his decisions eventually landed him in prison with a net worth of negative $100 million. In order to do that much damage while being completely incapacitated from drugs, he had to separate his wealth creation from his personal time to the ninety-ninth degree.

While Jordan had to be talented to build such a scheme, he quickly became blinded by his own wealth and ego. In short, while some very smart plays got him in a position of extreme wealth, he also made poor decisions that affected every other facet of life. If you have seen the movie, almost every decision he made besides the setup of the scheme was wrong. If he had just conserved in a few areas, he would have probably gotten away with the entire scam. But he made poor decision after poor decision and took actions without putting any thought into them.

This proves that even someone who makes poor decisions can become incredibly wealthy *if* he understands the pillars of wealth and how wealth is created.

Jordan might have been a scamming, idiot drug addict, but he understood the second pillar of wealth so well that those facts didn't matter. Jordan understood how to separate his time from making money, which led him to get rich quickly.

(Before we continue, I would just like to state I have a lot of respect for the man Jordan is today. He made some very poor choices during the time period I talked about above but was able to do a complete one-eighty and has some of the best sales training on the market today.)

So, to repeat myself and really drill this notion into your brains, a major key to getting rich is removing time from the equation. What exactly does this look like for you? Let me explain.

There is only one thing you have a finite amount of in a day: time. Donald Trump has the same amount of time as a man living on the street. And no matter who you are, you have twenty-four hours every single day to eat, sleep, work, exercise, learn a new skill, spend time with your family, sit around in traffic, binge-watch on Netflix, worry, procrastinate, and work toward a goal.

Because of this, there is a cap to the amount of work one person can do, and in effect, the amount of money that he or she will make. This leaves us with two choices.

CHOICE 1: INCREASE THE VALUE OF OUR TIME

This is what lawyers, pro athletes, and to a lesser extent, traffic fighters do. These people get paid per hour or per project. LeBron James is so talented that a minute of his time can be worth thousands of dollars. However, at the end of the day, LeBron only has so many minutes. Even though he can make an incredible amount of money, his income is capped.

Now, the problem with this mind-set is that in order for your time to be worth an insane amount of money, you have to be AMAZING at what you do. And, even if you're the best painter in your town or the best accountant in your state, other people decide what your time is worth (which I'll explain further in a few paragraphs).

First, being amazing is hard and many times out of our control. To be the best at something, you have to be incredibly talented and smart. Most of us are not incredibly talented and have an average IQ. We are genetically disqualified at birth. Your chances of becoming famous or becoming so exceptional at something to the point that your time is worth as much as LeBron James's time are slim at best. It's possible, but it's difficult and unlikely. However, this is how we are trained to think by our teachers, families, and colleagues. One hour of work equals X amount of dollars. One year of work equals X amount of dollars. Your life equals X amount of dollars.

Second, someone *else* has to deem your time's worth. If people suddenly stopped watching basketball, LeBron's boss would deem his time worthless and stop paying him millions a year. If your boss doesn't feel your time is worth more than $60,000 a year, he's not going to pay you more than $60,000 a year. Even if you set your own salary or wage as a freelancer or business owner, some people might decline your services because you are too expensive, which in effect means that other people decide what you are worth. Long story short, your income is generally in someone else's control. As this book continues, you will see that control is one of the most important concepts behind getting rich quickly.

None of this would be an issue if we had unlimited hours in our day to sell our products and services to people who are interested in them. However, we do not. And again, most of us are average, and our time is simply not worth that much. This means that the rest of us are doomed to a low-capped income due to limited time and a low value of our time. On top of that, no matter what we do, we can never generate more time, so our personal income as a solo worker is not scalable, so we cannot grow it as much as we want to.

If we still think that time equals money, getting rich quickly would be quite challenging. Luckily, we have another choice.

CHOICE 2: COMPLETELY SEPARATE TIME FROM INCOME

Jordan Belfort's sales pitch was unarguably pure genius. However, I doubt we would be talking about him right now if he didn't expand his business and spread this knowledge past his own brain. Even with an amazing sales pitch, if Jordan had kept himself to a one-man business, he would not have become so wealthy. It's as simple as that. This is because there are only so many phone calls he could make in a day and only so many clients he could manage by himself without help.

The reason he accumulated wealth so fast was because his first step was to vastly separate his time from his income, meaning his income wasn't solely based on his time alone. His time was limited and the value for his time could only be increased so much. In fact, he was only making around $70,000 a month when he was working as a one-man unit. This quickly multiplied to millions a month when he changed his business model to include more people (or, more accurately, cloned himself hundreds of times by passing his sales pitch on to them).

Because of this, when we want to get rich quickly, the first step is setting up a business in which we can separate our time from money. Instead of trying to increase the value of our time like many people do, we need to spend our time creating a machine like Jordan that generates income regardless of our time. Unlike you, your machine can work an almost infinite number of hours and complete an infinite amount of tasks thanks to employees and technology. A machine like his could make money while we sleep, while we're on vacation, and even while we're on a date with our spouse. In other words, you're not getting paid for the hours you work; you're getting paid while your machine works.

Instead of spending our time working, we should spend our time creating systems that do the work for us. This term is often referred to as passive income. Passive income is income that our machine generates once it is built and is completely separated from our time. In short, this means you will be generating money even if you're blackout drunk at a rock concert. Pretty cool idea, right? Here's an example.

HOW I SEPARATE MY TIME FROM MY BUSINESS/INCOME

The majority of my businesses are based around software. The ads that send people to my websites, the websites themselves, their sales and billing processes, and the actual software all run without me being there. Each part in this system took a significant amount of time to create. However, at this point they require very little time to maintain.

In fact, if I sell one hundred units or one million units, the difference in my time is very little. This is what enables me to sell an unlimited amount of units and generate virtually an unlimited amount of income. If my business required me to deal with every single customer, there is no way I could obtain such a high level of wealth because my time is capped, so the amount of people I could help is capped, which means my income would be capped. It doesn't, though. No matter what I am personally doing with my time, people will continually buy and be billed for my software.

In fact, the only thing that limits my income is the size of the market and how well my system sells to it. So, at this point, all I have to do is to make sure that my machine is working flawlessly. And, once it has maxed out my market, I can make other machines in other markets. This pillar and idea are really that simple.

In short, there is no limit to how much money I can make or how far and fast I can scale my business. This also means I can sell my business for tons of money . . . but more on that later on.

HOW TO SEPARATE YOUR TIME FROM YOUR BUSINESS/INCOME

When you start your first business, the value of your time will be extremely low . . . unless you are a recognized expert in some field. As you make more money, the value for your time will probably go up due to your expertise at generating money. But, for the moment, let's just assume your income is crap. Without a boss, employment, or any fame or recognition due to your expertise, your time is worth very little.

Because of this, you need to find a process that works and then clone yourself as fast as possible so this process can be repeated time and time again, whether you're personally involved or not (just like Jordan Belfort and I did).

Now, cloning ourselves and creating a machine can mean many things. A machine could simply be a website with an automated delivery system (which is very cheap to create). A machine could also be hiring sales people or employees to replicate a task. Separating time from money is not just one task, so you cannot view it as a single goal.

Your first goal when separating time from money is to simply find a process that works. For example, if you are trying to sell real estate, your first step is to create a sales process that works. Then, after you have a process that works, you need to find a way to separate your time by automating as much of your business as possible so that you're not being paid for the time you spend working.

Examples of this would be creating a website that manages client appointments, running ads that attract clients for you, and hiring other people to sell the real estate for you. That is a fairly simple system, but you can see how simple separating your time can be. At this point, if you manage to clone yourself just four times with four new employees, you can increase your income at least four times without lifting a finger.

Or, let's say you get into Internet marketing and buy ads promoting other people's products. And, for every product you sell, you get a 50 percent commission. If you manage to make this profitable, there are only so many ads you can manage and only so much income you can make. If you hire a staff to copy your advertising process into other markets, you can effectively double or triple your income for every staff member you add. You've created the first process to making money, and then you removed your time by cloning and automating this process.

Get it? Got it? Good. Now, instead of just talking about it, let's get into some real-world actionable steps you can take right now to bring this pillar into your life.

TIME TO CUT THE CRAP: HOW TO TURN THESE IDEAS INTO PRACTICAL STEPS

Want to know what I hate? When I open up a business book and all the author can offer me is ideas. For an idea or mind-set to be practical, there has to be real-world steps on how to execute and achieve it. Therefore, at the end of many chapters in this book I will include steps you can take to implement my ideas, whether you're a beginner in the business world or already own a successful company.

I will be doing this in every chapter that it is necessary. Some of the pillars can be applied as a beginner in the same fashion they can be applied as a veteran, but some must be done differently depending on where you are in your business. So, some pillars will have separate beginner and veteran tips, and some will not.

SEPARATING TIME FROM INCOME FOR A COMPLETE BEGINNER

If you are totally new to entrepreneurship, you are probably still wrapping your head around the fact that you can make money without actually working. The good news is that you can use this idea when planning your first business so you can do it the right way on your first try.

When starting your first business, the first step is deciding what type of business you would like to start. You might already have an idea, but if you don't, don't worry because we will address that later on in the book. The important thing to remember is that you *must* apply this mind-set to every business you start.

If you think of a potential business, you need to ask the following questions before you dive in:

1. Can this business make money while I am not present?
2. Can this moneymaking process be done by others or automated by machines?
3. If this business becomes successful, could I train someone else to run it?
4. Would it be possible to make the process of delivering on $100 in sales the same as delivering on $1 million in sales? Can I scale this business without having to increase my time involvement?

If your business idea can pass all those questions with a "Yes!" you may be onto something. If not, this is not a business that you should consider long term, because while a business that fails these questions *can* make you money, it will require greater and greater amounts of your time and lower your quality of life. Even worse, it will stop you from having the time to pursue other businesses that pass the above test and could prevent you from making more money in less time.

From now on, when you have an idea, run through those questions and see if you can imagine a way to format the business so that it passes the test. Some businesses that are usually based on your time can be arranged differently to create a time-free business. You just have to think a little harder and smarter when coming up with your business ideas.

IMPORTANT: Keep in mind that no business will be time free at the start. Most time-free businesses are much more time intensive at the start than time-required businesses. The key is to always create businesses that are moving towards a time-free business. The questions above will allow you to do this.

SEPARATING TIME FROM INCOME FOR A VETERAN BUSINESS OWNER

This is the million-dollar question right here. There are countless entrepreneurs that make hundreds of thousands a year but have to spend over sixty hours a week maintaining their businesses. Not only does this stop them from scaling and making multimillions, but it also stops them from having choices in their lives. While these people might own their businesses, they are slaves to them and the money they create. At no point can they let their businesses run themselves. This is a serious issue because separating money from time is *essential* to becoming truly wealthy and having a high quality of life.

For example, I had a friend who was making over $200,000 a month with his marketing business. However, he was the only person running it, and it involved massive amounts of his time. He could not make any more money because his time was maxed out. While he was making money, he was not free from money because his time controlled his business. He was working so much that he barely even had time to enjoy his money!

This is very common. You can see it with lawyers, doctors, chiropractors, marketing service providers, personal trainers, and the list goes on and on. The main reason they fail to get out of the vicious cycle is because they have no idea how to automate things or hand over the reins to other people, or they do not want to take away from their profits by hiring other people. To respond to this, I simply have a quick story that I always tell friends and strangers alike.

So there are two marketers, Joe and Nick. Both make $100,000 a month but want to make $200,000 a month.

Joe handles *everything*, because he's too stubborn to hire a staff. He works twelve-hour days and is proud of it. But, because he works twelve hours a day managing his business, a few things happen:

1. He's a pro marketer, but because his time is spent designing, supporting, coding, etc., he has very little time to focus solely on moving his business forward.
2. Because his time is split five different ways, the work being done can never really be the best of the best in any particular area. After all, he only has twelve hours a day.

Nick on the other hand takes $30,000 of his $100,000 a month and hires a developer ($10,000), a designer ($5,000), a support team ($5,000), and a content creator ($10,000) to help with his business.

Nick wakes up every Monday morning and sits down with his team to make sure they know exactly what to do. Just this simple conversation leads to over forty hours of total work combined from the staff every day versus Joe's twelve.

Even better, every part of Nick's business is handled by an expert in the field who is solely focused on that area, so the work is of much higher quality.

More so, Nick can spend his day thinking about how to improve the business and move it forward. So, instead of spending twelve hours a day managing, he spends eight hours a day focusing and advancing the business.

Now, at the end of the month, Joe (who does not take weekends off) has put 360 hours (twelve hours a day) into his business. At least half of that is spent just managing it.

On the other hand, Nick (who takes weekends off along with his staff) and his employees have been able to put 1,200 hours of expert work into his business.

Just looking at the math alone, Nick's business grows just because of the number of hours that go into, and his time spent growing the business is not as restricted as Joe's.

Nick continues to spend at least 30 percent of his earnings on adding to staff while the business grows, and within two years the business is making $1 million a month, and Nick is taking home at least $700,000 a month (after giving raises to his employees and hiring a few more if necessary), all while working normal hours.

He then sells the business for $50 million and retires. His time was never needed to make the business run successfully, so it was easy to sell.

Joe on the other hand gets his business to $200,000 a month, but it gets to the point where all his time is spent managing it, so it stalls there. Then, one of a few things will happen:

1. Joe is forced to work twelve-hour days forever. He can't sell his business because it's based around his time.
2. A competitor pops up who can move much faster than Joe and makes a superior product than Joe. He simply can't keep up and gets put out of business.
3. Joe takes a break for a few weeks. When he comes back, the business is losing money due to his lack of presence. One day, he is burnt out and takes a wee bit too long of a break and the whole business goes to shit due to a change in the marketplace.

Who would you rather be?

What you need to realize is that as a business owner (in almost all cases), intelligently spending substantial chunks of your earnings to grow your business almost always increases your overall profit. It is far better to have a profit margin of 30 percent on a business that can be scaled to $10 million a year and sold for tens of millions of dollars than to have 100 percent of an unsellable business that is plateauing at $200,000 a year.

What you must do is look at your business and pose a series of questions, which are similar to the beginner's questions but cater to people who already own businesses.

1. What part of my business can be automated by a staff or technology?
2. Is there a way to get people with my skill set to work for me and sell their time instead of mine?

3. What skill sets do I lack that are needed to grow this business, and what skill sets do my new employees need to possess?

Here are a few examples of how to apply these questions to self-run businesses.

Example A:

A highly respected chiropractor runs a practice that takes sixty hours a week to maintain $200,000 a year in income. He automates his service by opening a chiropractor clinic and hiring other chiropractors that he trains himself to keep the quality consistent. Then, he opens up multiple clinics under this brand. Lastly, he hires an advertising manager who will be responsible for attracting more clients.

He now has five clinics each with three chiropractors who generate $100,000 each a year in profit. He is now earning $1.5 million a year without having to treat a single patient.

This same format can be applied to many other professions such as lawyers, massage therapists, and marketing specialists.

Example B:

A famous burger chef works eighty hours a week to keep his restaurant at $200,000 a year in profits. He has a great brand and amazing recipes. He decides to sell his brand and create a chain. He also automates the sales of all these chains via an automated online delivery system. In return for 40 percent in royalties, these chains get to use his brand, recipes, and delivery system.

This burger chef now has two hundred chain locations, each making him $10,000 a month in income. He is now making $2 million a month without frying up a single burger.

Get the picture? With proper automation and business planning, any time-intensive business can become a time-separate moneymaking machine. Even if you are already entrenched ir

THE 10 PILLARS OF WEALTH

time-intensive business, there are simple ways to separate your time from your income.

IT'S TIME TO TAKE BACK YOUR TIME

Time is the only thing you can never generate more of, and every human has the exact same amount of in a day. To become wealthy, you have to learn how to generate more time by hiring people (and/or building machines), using their time as your own, and using your time to grow the business. If you look at the most profitable businesses in the world, the owner's time is usually so separated that he does not even have to be there. Every successful person I know understands this, and the richest are the ones who abuse it. In fact, the richest people in the world make money from their money and have zero time involvement. Bill Gates, for example, makes billions from his investments, letting his dollars generate money for him. His time is not a factor in the businesses that make him millions. If you don't separate your time from your income, it will be nearly impossible for you to become as wealthy as you desire.

Keep this in mind so you can keep your time.

THE 3RD PILLAR

ACCEPTING THAT YOU MUST BE BETTER THAN EVERYONE ELSE

In this chapter, to get my point across I want to talk about a little racing industry you may have heard of: NASCAR.

Now, what I want you to imagine is that you are teleported to another universe where you are an up-and-coming NASCAR driver. You have also magically been given the talents of a top driver. Now keep imagining the following with me . . .

For some odd reason, the NASCAR sponsors love you. You have the most advanced car, the best pit crew, and your car has illegal additions that make it go 2 mph faster than every other car (which is actually HUGE when it comes to racing). In real life, illegal additions are not commonplace. But let's imagine that you are so freaking cool that nobody at NASCAR cares.

Everything is stacked in your favor, except that you have one problem: you have low self-esteem and you truly don't think you are going to win, which makes you afraid to drive fast and take the risk. In fact, you think you are pretty average and that you are anything but a winner. You're not even sure why you're in this scenario in the first place.

The question I have for you in this scenario is: Even with your advantages, do you believe that you will be the one racer to win? With ninety-nine other drivers, that would literally put you in the 1 percent.

Think about it for a second.

If there is an opening that is slightly risky, are you going to take it? No, because you think that you are average and don't have faith that you will make it.

If it comes to a point in the competition where you are racing neck and neck with three other racers, are you going to push yourself harder to beat them or slow down to stay safe? You will likely panic and slow down, because you don't believe you have the skills to compete. If you tried to pass them, you might spin out of control, or worse—hit one of the other cars. It's better to stay safe than to deal with the consequences of trying hard, right? WRONG.

During the entire race, are you going to take on challenges and make moves that a great racer would take? Nope! You are you going to try to go for the smoothest, most consistent route and hope you get lucky enough to win.

Does this seem harsh? Are you getting angry with me and thinking, "Alex, I'm not that type of person. I *do* work hard, but I always fail." Well, the harsh truth is that you probably wouldn't need to read this book if your fear of failure and desire for comfort weren't holding you back from success. Building your business must be your number-one priority in life for you to actually succeed. If it's not your number-one priority, that's okay. But you have to accept the fact that it is very unlikely that you will become a multimillionaire. Instead of making excuses all the time, just admit to yourself that family or comfort or being lazy or living a "normal" life are bigger priorities than becoming wealthy.

Back to the story. You can see just by what I have laid out above that, even with all the advantages in the world, you will not succeed if you do not believe you will succeed. If you think you will win the race, you are likely to win it. If you think there ance in hell that you will win the race, I can guarantee you will not win unless the other ninety-nine cars get y lightning at the same exact time. Having the skills tools to win won't mean squat unless you believe you are in the top 1 percent. You have to believe you are elite, and in your heart of hearts you must think you are better than your competitors. If you don't, you will not make the choices and take the opportunities needed to beat them and win.

My questions for you are: Do you think you are great? Do you have advantages that others do not have? If you were in a room with ninety-nine other people trying to do what you do, would you be the best, smartest, most competent, most capable person in the room?

If your answer is no, or even a hesitant yes, I am sorry, but you are 100 percent screwed. Statistically, only 1.1 percent of households are considered millionaires. (And way less than 1 percent of individuals are considered millionaires.)

By wanting to become wealthy, you are also saying that you want to accept the challenge to be better at making money than 99 percent of the people on this planet. Just by attempting this, you are going to have to accept the fact that you must not just be good, you must be incredible. If you think differently, then you are done before you even get started. If you are part of the 99 percent and never change your belief system, all this book will be is amusing, wishful toilet reading.

If you asked me those questions from a few paragraphs ago, my answer to all of them 100 percent of the time would be a confident Yes. I *know* that I am extraordinarily good at what I do and that I'm better at making money than 99 percent of people in this world. I can think quicker, move faster, and bring better ideas to my market than almost any human being I've ever met.

I can statistically prove this, too. I knew hundreds of people when I was in middle school. Out of these people, I am the only millionaire. If you grabbed one hundred people in my school and put us in a money Hunger Games, I would brutally kill them all. Better yet, if you took every single person in my school and had them compete against me in what I personally do to make money, they would not stand a chance at surpassing me.

I am unembarrassed to admit that yes, I am better than 99 percent of people at making money. Now, don't confuse confidence with cockiness. I know what I am capable of, and this confidence is what has allowed me to be successful in the first place. If I was the NASCAR driver in my earlier example, I would take every chance I got to win the race because I truly believe I am the best out of the one hundred drivers and I can handle whatever comes my way.

And that simple thought right there is immensely powerful and almost all that is needed to eventually make money. The belief that you are great, and accepting the fact that you must be great, is the third pillar. In fact, if you only remember one pillar from this whole book, make sure it's this one. As you will see in the rest of this chapter, this pillar can be powerful enough to create massive wealth. But, without the support of the other pillars, it almost always leads to a massive loss of wealth.

THE BIGGEST THING HOLDING PEOPLE BACK IS BELIEVING THEY ARE AVERAGE OR NOT GOOD ENOUGH

I tell people all the time what I do and how I make money. I also tell them ways they can make money pretty easily. I tell them that anyone can become wealthy with the right belief system and the right tools. Then, I give them ideas on how to create wealth.

I tell them to make software.

"Oh, but I don't know how to code."

I tell them to learn how to sell and to just sell something, anything.

"Oh, well, I'm uncomfortable selling."

I tell them to start an online business.

"I'm not good at Internet stuff like you."

Yes, these are real responses from real people who think they are average, not smart enough, or not capable enough to conquer challenges. These kinds of people don't believe they can accomplish anything because they don't think they deserve it. Because of this, they never act or take risks and, because of that, they never reach their goals. They simply continue their lives as average "traffic fighters" who never become wealthy.

However, if you truly believe you are great, everything changes. What if we tell a person who thinks they are (or deserve to be) in the 1 percent the same things we told people in the 99 percent?

You should make software.

"I don't know how to code, but I can definitely learn how to, or at the very least, find a way to pay a developer to make software for me."

You should learn how to sell.

"Selling makes me really uncomfortable, but I can learn to overcome that and become a sales machine."

You should start an online business.

"Man, I don't even know how people make money online. But if other people can do it, then I sure as hell can learn how to do it too."

The funny thing about this is that the person in this example could be a total misguided idiot, but since he thinks he is great and capable, he will take actions that the former person never would. If he changes his life so that every action he takes and every thought he has leads to accomplishing his goals, then nothing can stop him from doing just that. Then, one day, he will be successful enough that hundreds, thousands, or even millions of other people will agree that he is great and capable.

As you can see, having this simple belief can make a moron rich, and lacking it can make a genius poor. Every day, I turn on the TV and see average (or below average) people getting rich with average ideas. The only thing that separates them from other average people is the belief that they can do it. It happens all the time. Just walk around a mall and look at all the stupid ideas that are flying off the shelves. Heck, just watch an episode of Shark Tank and look at some of the horrible ideas that float through there that sometimes get invested in. Guess what? As stupid as some of those ideas are, those people truly believe in themselves, and that belief will lead them to future success.

Remember the Snuggie? What about mood rings, or that creepy fish plaque that sings? All stupid ideas (or brilliant ideas, depending on how you look at it) that made people millions of dollars. At the end of the day, this pillar is that damn powerful. In fact, it is even more powerful in the hands of a fool, because they are able to blind themselves from this thing called "logic" and are eager to take risks and chances that no sane person would ever take.

On the other end of this spectrum, every once in a while there are stories about super millionaires losing all their money. I know a guy who sold his business for $70 million and bought an island. But, two years later, he was back working an eight-to-five job because he went bankrupt. The reason this happens is they lack the rest of the pillars I will cover in this book. You can see how powerful this belief/pillar can be at creating wealth, but it can also destroy wealth if you don't possess the others. Even a moron can get lucky with an idea, but they rarely stay rich if they do not smarten up.

The reason that I keep saying words like "moron" and "idiot" is because these are the people that are so blinded by faith that they pursue goals no one in their right mind would go for. They chase things that only a fool or moron would. I am sure you have a friend that is constantly chasing some dream despite what everyone is saying. Or even better, I am sure you know someone that is blindly confident in themselves even though their track record of success is awful.

The thing is, these morons are also generally pretty confident, because they don't know any better. And you know what? That is an awesome trait. That's why inventions that seem silly become million-dollar ideas . . . because the inventor believed in himself and worked hard at making his dream a reality. But, as I just mentioned, these confident morons won't stay successful very long unless they learn and apply the rest of the pillars in this book.

I am going to go ahead and assume that you are not a moron and that you will take to heart the rest of the pillars in this book. However, everything I just covered prior to this backs up the necessity of the "greatness" pillar. What we want to do is adopt the blind confidence of a moron while adopting the practicality of a rocket scientist. Sometimes you simply have to ignore common sense and give in to blind faith. This is something that average people cannot do, and therefore they can never bet on themselves and move forward if there is any chance of risk.

YOU MUST BELIEVE YOU ARE GREAT

Now look, this is not some hippie self-help book where I tell you, "If you just think about something hard enough, it will happen." There is a very scientific, mathematical reason why this pillar has such an impact. It comes down to what I like to call the BLR (Belief, Actions, and Results) system.

As I have stated many times in this book, beliefs drive our actions. If you believe that you are extremely good looking, it will cause you to act more confident around the opposite sex and, well, I don't have to explain to you what the result is in this scenario. By being confident, you will take certain actions and those actions will get you results (good or bad).

So, how do you get the result of incredible wealth? You create a business that is better than 99 percent of other businesses. And how do you create a great and successful business?

The answer: You *believe* and *accept* the fact that you have to be great.

Our entire lives, we are told that we are not going to be great (not in this way, at least). In fact, throughout our lives most of our teachers and mentors convince us that we outright suck at life and teach us how to prepare for the worst by taking the traffic fighter life stance.

Seriously, has a teacher ever told you that you had a good chance of being super rich and buying your own island? Let's all say it together: "NEVER." If they were praising you for a job well done, they probably said something like, "You're so smart. You're going to get into a great college," or, "You'll make a great lawyer one day." And while your teacher's intentions were probably good, these words convinced you that becoming a traffic fighter means that you are actually succeeding. (This is true for some people. If you wanted to grow up and become a lawyer and now you are a partner at a practice, then you are successful because you reached your goal. Or if you wanted to become a teacher and now you're a teacher, that is success as well. But, that's not what we're talking about here. If you are reading this book, I assume that you want overwhelming wealth and the massive success that comes with being a top 1 percent entrepreneur.)

Your teachers, both your in-school teachers and your out-of-school mentors, told you that the best possible thing you can do after high school is to attend a good college. They never explained that becoming rich is something you can strategically do without worrying about college or a typical eight-to-five job. (They themselves are not rich, so why would they convince you to do something that they themselves weren't able accomplish?)

Because of this, when people want to be rich, they do two things:

1. They stop themselves before they even begin. They don't believe they are great or deserve wealth, so they don't even try to succeed.
2. They try to become rich while still being average. They do not take on challenges, they play it safe, and they never leave their comfort zone (much like the NASCAR driver in the metaphor at the beginning of this chapter).

Both of these paths prevent people from becoming rich. The good news is that there is a way to overcome these obstacles, which is what this whole chapter is about. Can you guess it? Say it with me: "I must believe and accept the fact that I am great."

For example, you might not believe you are great when presented with a challenge like selling software. In fact, it might make you downright uncomfortable, so much so that you might not want to do it at all. You might even know how to start, but you never do because you think success is out of your reach.

However, this is where the power of *accepting the necessity of greatness* comes in. When you are feeling this way, simply step back and tell yourself that you are going to have to become great. Accept the fact that you are going to have to work hard and become really fucking good at whatever niche you choose.

Once you accept this, it becomes very clear what you need to do. All you have to do is whatever it takes to become great (yes, it's that easy). If that involves learning a whole new skill set, hiring a dozen people, or selling to people twelve hours a day six days a week until you become an expert at it, so be it. Eventually, if you work hard enough at something, you will become good—dare I say great—at it. Then it will be much easier to accept the fact that you *are* great.

If you spend ten years trying to master making money, it's almost impossible for you to not become an excellent businessperson.

One of my most successful friends has a net worth north of $500 million (probably closer to $700 million or $1 billion by the time this book is published). His name is Com.

When Com started his first software business, he didn't know a single thing about writing code or running a business. He was actually a high school dropout with virtually no experience doing anything. Most people thought he had no business starting a business. With that being said, Com always wanted to be an entrepreneur. And, even though he had no idea how to become successful, he just accepted the fact that you have to overcome a lot of obstacles on your way to success. Com knew nothing, but he accepted that he would have do whatever it took to become great.

Earlier I explained that if you spend ten years confidently pushing yourself forward, you would eventually become great at something. I consider myself a bad example of this, because my first business was actually profitable, and my second official business is now worth well over $20 million. With Com, though, this was not the case. Com's first eight businesses went bankrupt and caused him severe financial hardship. Com is one of the most ambitious and driven people I know, but we can safely assume that Com did not have what it took (at the time) to overcome the obstacles that he faced. Because he understood and accepted the fact that he would have to become great to overcome his hurdles, he just kept moving forward.

(Note: Earlier in this book, I state that you can start a business with low risk and low investment yet still obtain a high ROI. While that *is* the safer and better way, and that *is* what I suggest, that is not what Com did. He created his wealth by attempting to hit home runs at every swing of the bat, which luckily worked out for him eventually. That's not the point of this story, though.)

Take a step back and look at this, though. I hear people bitch and moan that they can't start a business because of little things like "not understanding the Internet" or "being bad at selling." These are not real disadvantages; they are opinions that can be changed or areas of interest that can be learned. And these complaints start to sound a little ridiculous when you see the blatant, *real* disadvantages that were in Com's way.

He was bankrupt *and* had a zero-for-eight record when it came to starting a business. If you looked at him on paper, he would have been the horse at the races with the 1/82 odds. Who would want to work for or invest in a person with those odds? The answer: No one. And that's exactly what Com had to deal with.

If you want to hear the full story, check out my YouTube channel (Google "Alex Becker YouTube Com Mirza Interview"), but for now, let me tell you the abridged version. After eight failures, Com started a gambling business. Shortly after this business launched, he learned that it was going to get shut down by legal regulations unless he could come up with over 1 million pounds (he was in the UK) in capital. (This is what I'm talking about as a *real* problem/disadvantage.)

Com, again, accepted that in order to become great, he would have to do whatever it takes. After being rejected by almost every investment source in the UK, Com was able to secure the investment by literally knocking door to door around an office building after being thrown out of his final investment meeting. And, if that wasn't difficult and stressful enough, he got the money within hours of the legal deadline.

A few years later, Com sold his stake in this business for hundreds of millions of dollars (by US dollar-to-pound conversion) and was actually one of the first investors in MySpace. He is also currently one of the most successful investors in the world.

The point is that Com was not great. In fact, in the real world, he was seen as a complete failure. But he kept working and learning and pushing year after year, failure after failure, because he accepted the difficulty of becoming great and kept ultimate faith in himself that he would become successful. It took him a while, but he got there despite all the disadvantages he dealt with.

Do you think his journey would have been possible if he had not believed he was great? Do you think he would have taken all those risks repeatedly if he considered himself average? The truth is, Com had the worst car on the track, yet still drove like he believed he was the best driver on the track. Not only did he leap to the 1 percent, he leapt to the .001 percent of the pack.

None of this would have happened without the acceptance that he had to become great and the eventual belief that he wa great. He would have gotten an eight-to-five job and surrendered to the "traffic fighters" life of mediocrity after his third failure. Heck, most people don't even need to reach failure to give up on their dreams. He hit it eight times and still didn't give up!

This is how powerful this pillar is in a person's life. Now, with *just* this pillar, you can become immensely rich, but blind faith in yourself without the other pillars to support you will almost always lead to losing your wealth. So, do not confuse taking blind risks with embracing this pillar. In order to truly become successful, you have to embrace this pillar with all your being while remembering the others. On top of this, when you combine this pillar with the others, you can become wealthy without taking blind risks, because you will understand how money works. Once you learn about money and business, these risks will actually become opportunities.

Desiring to be wealthy means that you are aiming to be anything but average. You are actually working towards being better at making money than almost every other being on the planet. There's no room for people that do not believe in themselves. You can't sneak into the top 1 percent with skills or ideas alone. You must have the whole package, which is why you need all ten pillars to truly get to the top.

As I have said many times, the biggest issue isn't understanding this pillar, it's believing and applying this pillar.

Here's how you do it.

WEALTH GENERATION FOR BEGINNERS

If you are brand new to this train of thought, this chapter probably seems like a bunch of unnecessary garbage. But, as I already explained, thinking that you're great doesn't instantly put $5 your bank account, and skills alone won't generate h either. You need to believe, act, and make decisions he idea that you are already great. But how do you do 're just starting out in the business world?

You need to think about the actions you would take if you were already great and successful. When you run into a problem, you need to ask yourself the question, "If I were a freak-of-nature genius business master capable of anything in the world, how would I handle this situation?"

Is this over the top? Yes. However, if you run into a problem and ask this question, it's virtually impossible to say "I can't," or, "I don't know how to do that." For example, whenever I tell people to start an online business, all I hear are "buts:"

- But I can't code.
- But I'm not good at talking to people.
- But I don't know how to do X, Y, and Z.

You probably think the exact same way. You are probably reading this book and thinking, "This is great info and all, but this Becker guy is good at all these things that I am not. That's why he's successful and that's why I'm not successful." And yes, this is true; you stink right now.

However, if you apply the question I laid out above, this does not matter. This question will lead you to the exact same actions that any super millionaire would take in your position. If you want to start a business but are bad at communicating with strangers, simply ask the question, "What would a successful person do?" Suddenly, it will become brutally apparent that you have no option but to become a skilled communicator. (Learning how to become a skilled communicator is the next step you must take, but knowing what you need to do is the key here.)

It doesn't have to be anything drastic, but this thought process will get you moving in the direction of greatness. Instead of saying "Screw it. I suck at communicating with people, so I better keep my day job," you will begin searching on Google how to improve your speaking and writing skills. Then, you will start taking action on what you learn.

Now, when you take action based on the answers this question brings you, you will eventually start getting some wins.

You will make your first $100, then your first $1,000, and then suddenly you will start thinking "Yes, I can do this." Over time, you will not have to ask yourself, "What would a great person do?" because you will turn into a great person and naturally gain complete faith in yourself. You will instinctively start going for the kill and believing you can get the kill, resulting in you actually getting the kill.

WEALTH GENERATION FOR VETERANS

Maybe you're a person who has already had a few successes in business, but you're currently at a plateau. Maybe you're getting crushed by new competitors. Or maybe you haven't gotten a new client in a few weeks and don't know why. Perhaps you just want more money and have no idea how to get it. More often than not, the reason for all these issues is that you are competent at what you do but not great at what you do.

I see this all the time with business owners. In fact, most of the time business owners know in the back of their heads what they need to do, but they fail to do it. Their competitors have better branding, higher quality products, etc., so how can they compete?

The obvious solution is to take their business to the next level. However, people fail to do this because they believe they cannot be great. They believe that they have limits and that there are just some things that they can't do as well as other people can.

Just to make sure I drill this important message into your brain, I am going to repeat what I said in the beginner's section: The *only* solution to this problem is to eliminate limits from your thought process and ask yourself, "What would a great entrepreneur do to move forward in this situation?" This will allow you to see it from a completely different angle to figure out the best solution for your problem.

I constantly meet entrepreneurs that are making $10,000 to $15,000 a month in profit. Yes, this is decent money, but they cannot figure out how to make more. The reason for this is because they simply refuse to evolve. They will ask how they can get a business like mine or someone else's at my level. They are looking for some tactic or secret that will allow them to remain average but let them make money as if they were great.

The true answer to this question is, "You have to be great to have a business like mine." You need to put an extreme amount of time and investment into:

- Improving your brand.
- Improving your marketing.
- Improving your product.
- Improving every single thing you do.

For example, I once hit a point where I was making money but had serious trouble scaling my business. I would see businesses in the same niche as mine making ten times more than I was making, and it would upset me because I didn't know how to get my business to that point.

Then I realized that I had to be great. I had to be better than who I was, and better than them. To do that, I had to:

- Outwork them.
- Bring superior people into my company.
- Master marketing my business.

This seems like simple logic, but before this realization, I would tell myself:

- You don't have a staff like they have.
- You don't know how to make software like they do.
- You aren't a master of advertising.
- You are afraid to lose money.

After admitting to myself that I have to be great to succeed, my thoughts shifted to:

- I need to master making software.
- I need to hire a superior staff.
- I need to learn advertising.

And instead of sitting around looking at "cannots," I started figuring out how to make the above things happen. It pushed me out of my comfort zone and I had to invest money into my company that I would usually keep for myself. The result, however, was that my business grew substantially. Great business people do not sit in their comfort zone; they push things to the next level, even if it means a bit of hardship.

Again, this mind-set is not for a broke newcomer to business. This is for someone who already has some money but wants to make *a lot* of money. Your issue will almost always be sitting in your comfort zone and refusing to be the absolute best at what you do. If you simply sit down and admit to yourself that you need to be the best regardless of the investment or time involved, you will have a hard time staying in that comfort zone.

If your goal is to make money in your business, but being the best isn't an equal goal, then you probably won't stay in business very long or won't be able to grow your business to its full potential. This is because you are so focused on money that you might not want to spend any on necessary investments to grow your business. To be the best, you have to make investments and beat other business owners. This takes time, money, and doing things other business owners will not.

Accept that fact and execute it no matter how uncomfortable it makes you. Then, becoming great will be inevitable.

MOVING IN THE DIRECTION OF GREATNESS RESULTS IN GREATNESS

What you will see many times in this book is that repeated actions are all it takes to achieve desired goals. The only major hindrance is that actions are controlled by beliefs. The belief that you are great will result in great actions. The belief that you are average will result in average actions.

This is an undeniable fact from which you cannot escape. This is why this pillar of wealth is so essential. There can be no great actions without great thoughts. Even if you have everything in the world going for you, without the proper actions you will never win the race of wealth.

Like I have stated many times, having one pillar without the others is a recipe for disaster. If you truly live out this pillar without also living out the others, you will end up falling into the pits that have stripped so many millionaires of their wealth.

Thinking you are great without understanding how to control money will undoubtedly result in making bad decisions. This is where our next pillar comes into play.

———————— THE 4TH PILLAR
KNOWING EVERY LITT
IS 100% YOUR FA

Warning: This chapter is going to start off in a pretty dark place, and I will more than likely piss you off. I am going to take this example to the extreme so that you *fully* grasp what I am trying to teach you. So, to explain what this pillar is about, let me tell you a story about a man named Steven.

(Before reading this, please keep in mind that this is just a story I use to drive my point home. This is not a judgment, and this does not reflect my personal feelings towards a situation like this. This is an example, and only an example. So, please read this story objectively and not from a judgmental point of view. Thank you in advance!)

So, Steven is a youth pastor at a local church. From society's standards, he is pretty much the perfect guy. He has a polite and beautiful family and lives in a three-bedroom house with an actual white picket fence. He does not curse, he does not drink, and he donates one quarter of his annual salary to charity.

One night, Steven picks up his daughter from a sleepover at 12:00 a.m. because she became ill. After picking up his daughter, he drives home the way he always does. This way involves him driving very close to an IHOP, where college students usually go to eat after getting drunk at the bars.

He comes to an intersection that has a bit of a blind spot, but he looks both ways before proceeding. Everything looks clear, and there is no way a car going normal speed could hit him even if the car was hidden in the blind spot. He then pulls out the intersection. At that very moment, a drunk college kid in a huge truck comes whipping around the blind spot at one hundred miles per hour and smashes into Steven's tiny Honda Civic. Steven and his daughter die on impact. The college kid has a bump on his head and is able to walk away from the accident.

Pretty messed up, right? But this leads me to a question with an answer you are not going to like. Whose fault was it that this happened?

The answer: It was Steven's fault . . . and he could have prevented it.

In our society, the fault is put on the drunk driver. We can point the finger at him all day long, put him in jail, and ruin his life. We can pass laws to prevent drunk driving and easily blame the drunk driver on this tragic accident. Everyone knows drunk driving can lead to horrible accidents, and drunk drivers are always seen as the bad guys.

At the end of the day though, who paid the price? Steven or the drunk driver? The cold hard truth is that Steven is the one who died and paid the ultimate price for the driver's actions. Sure, we can blame the drunk driver, but it doesn't change who loses in this situation. Blame doesn't change actions. Legally and personally, the driver should pay, but it isn't going to change the fact that Steven and his daughter are dead. (Once again, I know this seems incredibly harsh, but I have a point here. Just keep reading.)

Now, here is the problem with blaming other people or factors. When you do this, you release responsibility and control over your life. You are saying that there is no way you could have stopped it. By admitting this, you are letting bad things happen to you because you are deciding that they're not under your control. It's up to someone else or something else and it's their fault. More times than not, especially in business, the only person who pays the price is *you*, just like Steven was the one who paid the price in this story. (Yes, the drunk driver probably went to jail forever, but that doesn't bring Steven and his daughter back to life. So even if the person who is technically guilty does get punished, it doesn't negate what happened to you.)

WHAT IF STEVEN TOOK THE BLAME FOR EVERYTHING THAT HAPPENED TO HIM?

Let's reverse time and imagine that Steven thought like this. Imagine if he left the house thinking:

"It's late at night, and I'm driving near a popular drunk hangout spot. If I get hit by a drunk driver, it's my fault because I know that this option is possible but also avoidable. How can I prevent it from happening?"

His actions would have been drastically different. Here are a few things he could have done:

1. Convinced his daughter to stay the night at her friend's house.
2. Not driven by that IHOP where drunk college kids hang out.
3. Assumed that the blind spot would have a crazy driver and picked another route home.

The list goes on and on. Would this have been a bit paranoid? Yes! But if Steven had been a little more paranoid, he would have taken the fate of his daughter and himself out of the drunk driver's hands and placed it in his own. By the way, should the drunk driver blame himself? Yes, of course; it is 100 percent his fault since he was drunk and he hit Steven's car. He should blame himself because he could have prevented the accident, just like Steven should blame himself because he could have prevented the accident. But who would you rather be, the person who is dead but blame-free or the person who is alive but accepts all the blame?

I'm sorry for bringing up such an extreme example, but this is exactly how you have to start viewing the world in order to become rich. In order to generate wealth, you have to control wealth. And in order to control it, you have to take as much control of it from other people and factors as you can. The more responsibility you accept, the more control you have over your business.

In our society, we have been poisoned with a victim mentality. Everything is someone else's fault. It's your boss's fault, it's the economy's fault, it's a software malfunction's fault, it's anyone or anything else's fault but your own.

This mind-set will get you wiped out faster than anything when you are trying to become wealthy. Why? Because even if a bad situation is someone else's fault "in theory," you are the one who loses money and faces losing your wealth and success.

Let me repeat that again. In business, no matter whose "fault" it is, you will be the one who pays the price. The only way to prevent this is by always pointing the finger at yourself so you think about ways to take control away from other people or variables.

So, think about it. Where do you want the responsibility for fault (a.k.a. control) to be? Do you want your employee, the economy, or whatever other random factor to ruin your future and also get the blame? Wouldn't you rather accept responsibility for factors that are someone else's fault and fix them before they ruin something you value?

Let me explain this with real-world examples.

HOW I PERSONALLY LEARNED THIS PILLAR

A business I own earns between $500,000 and $1,000,000 a year. It was run by two of my employees at one point, and in the past I had repetitive issues with one employee. When I had these issues, I would blame him, threaten his job, and take money out of his paycheck. I thought this was the best way to handle this situation, and I blamed him for the mistakes he was making.

Well, one day I hired a person to audit our entire system. He let me know that several of our accounts had not received any service whatsoever. While this was a super small sample of our customer base, there was over $20,000 in billed orders that this employee simply had not fulfilled.

When confronted, the employee blamed the system he had been given, the software he had to work with, and everything except the fact that he had just not done his job. He did have some legitimate reasons (excuses), but all of these errors could have been prevented or fixed through simple actions.

At the end of the day, though, do you think the employee had to pay or compensate these people $20,000? Hell no. He got fired and was able to walk away with his prior paychecks and without debt to the business. I, on the other hand, had to contact my customers and make sure everyone was compensated.

Was this the employee's fault? If I had a victim mentality, sure. He didn't do his job and he screwed up the business. He should have done his job better and done what he was paid to do.

What good does that do me, though? The true fault lies with *me*. If I had accepted the mind-set that every single thing in my business is my responsibility, this never would have happened. I would be $20,000 richer and I would have kept all those customers I lost.

The sad truth is that we all know in the back of our heads that blaming others is a waste of time. The reason we do this is because it's easy. It is nice to have a scapegoat instead of looking in the mirror and blaming ourselves. It's far simpler to get mad at someone else and blindly hate them than taking a hit to our own ego. The fact of the matter is, though, that getting emotional and placing blame on others is a waste of time. It doesn't fix any problem and it doesn't make the past go away. The only thing it does is free us from blame, and that might make us feel guilt free, but feeling guilt free does not fix any issue. Accepting blame and fixing the problem does.

(An easy way to differentiate between a beginner entrepreneur and a seasoned one is to see how they handle situations when an employee or client does something wrong. If they complain and blame the other party, they're probably new at this whole business thing. If they barely mention the issue and immediately find a way to fix it, then you know these guys are pros.)

So, how would I have prevented the situation I had with the guilty employee if I had taken responsibility for my whole entire business in the first place? I would have:

- Made sure the employee's software was 100 percent effective and working.
- Checked his system once a week.
- Checked his work daily.
- Fired the employee once I noticed he was slacking off.

All these simple actions would have stopped this horrible situation from happening. But I chose to place the blame on my employee's shoulders and not my own. But, as you can hopefully see by now, placing the blame on anyone but myself was pointless because I was the one who still paid the price.

The more you adopt this line of thinking, the more you truly control (generating and protecting) your income.

Another example of this was during one of my many software openings. I release new software on a regular basis, and during my first few openings, everything went wrong. The hosting messed up, there were billing issues, and it was an overall giant cluster of awful.

At this time, I blamed the host and cursed my developers to hell. But again, the true fault was mine. Now when I open new software, I don't fault my host or the developers. I put it all on me. I am obnoxiously anal with checking every possible thing that could go wrong and, because of this, I control my success. It's not in my developer's hands because I am constantly checking their work. And, if it's not up to par, I fire them quickly so that I can find a developer who will meet my standards. It's not my software's or host's fault, because I test these to the extreme beforehand and only move forward when they are up to my standards—in other words, perfect.

Please note: Issues will always happen, and chasing perfection can often lead to "perfection paralysis," which is talked about in the sixth pillar. This is when you never complete anything because you're always waiting for it to be perfect. Sometimes, though, you have to push forward in order to make money, even if things are not 100 percent perfect. The point I'm trying to make here is that by accepting blame, I can prevent 90 percent of all possible issues and 99 percent of BIG issues before they happen.

The cold, hard truth is that no person or factor cares if you become rich or not. They do not give two shits about your level of income, as long as they are receiving a paycheck from you every two weeks. More so, the world does not care if you get rich, and it does not care if you work hard and have a good heart. So you have to focus on you because the only person in the world who is going to cover your ass all the time is, you guessed it, *you*. You can either place the blame on a world that doesn't give a shit about you, or you can put the blame on yourself (whom you hopefully care about a great deal). At the end of the day, the world will never pick up the tab for its mistakes, so you might as well accept the blame because you're going to be doing the work anyway.

This is why so many people think business is risky. It is because they do not accept blame. If you really cross your *t*'s and dot your *i*'s, there is a much lower chance that you will fail, because you can make good decisions and protect yourself.

HOW TO CHANGE YOUR MIND-SET AND ADOPT THIS PILLAR

You see, when you start to view everything as your fault, you start thinking in an extremely proactive way. You start thinking in actions instead of hoping for things to work out. This mind-set is pure, unrestricted power because it allows you to take control of your future away from the world and give it to yourself.

This is why this pillar is so important. The only problem is that it can be hard to bring into your life after so many years of having a victim mentality, which has poisoned your brain. Your brain does not want to give this up, because facing reality is extremely uncomfortable.

But, what if the reason you are average is not the fault of:

- Your teachers . . .
- Your parents . . .
- Your country . . .
- Your education . . .
- Your background . . .

. . . and is solely your fault? Well, for most people, it 100 percent is. Don't get me wrong; if you were born missing half your brain or with some other birth defect . . . then no, it's not your fault. But if you are reading this right now and you are poor or frustrated, then wake up, buddy—you suck and it's your fault! If you want to stop being awful at life, stop pointing the finger at whatever is stopping you from doing X, Y, and Z. You need to look in the mirror and point the blame at the whiny coward looking back at you.

Now, whether you are a beginner at generating wealth or you are a veteran, here is how you can incorporate this into your life and take back your power *today*.

GAINING CONTROL AS A NEWCOMER OF WEALTH

As always in this book, I am going to be blunt with you. Your life is probably full of disappointments. You don't make as much money as you want, you haven't achieved any of your dreams, and outside of your friends and family, you have no real value to anyone. Wherever you work, you might be liked, but you are ultimately just a money-generating employee that can be replaced at the drop of a hat.

You don't have the education, training, motivation, or whatever it takes to make money. No opportunities have ever come your way, and the world is just unfair to you. Or maybe you tried and failed because of some reason that you "can't control."

If you had what some successful so-and-so had, you could do it. But you don't, so you can't.

Guess what? This is all your fault, which means that *you* can change it. Maybe you got a bad roll of the dice in a few areas in life, but nothing is stopping you from continuing to roll the dice until you win.

Right now, I want you to write down everything you want in your life and then list why you don't have it. Do it. Right now. Go ahead.

Next, I want you to look at the list and then look at the "why" section. To get these things in your life, you need to take back your life from these "whys," a.k.a. these things or people or situations on which you're placing blame for your failures.

For example, maybe you wrote down that you wanted a large business, but don't have time because of work and family. How can you change this?

You could:

- Quit your job.
- Lower your bills substantially so you can afford to live more frugally.
- Work at nighttime after your family has gone to bed.
- Set strict hours and goals; for example, work three hours a night until you are making $3,000 a month and then quit your job to devote more hours to your business.

Tiny rant: I see this all the time. People want to start a business, but they cannot leave their current job because their lifestyle is too expensive. News flash: get a cheap apartment and a cheap, beat-up car, and you can live off $600 a month if you wanted. If you want major change in your life, you cannot be living the same life you have right now. That might be extreme if you have a family or student loans, but there are almost definitely a few expenses that you could cut back on. Spend less money at the grocery store, stop going out to eat, don't buy new clothes for the next six months, shop at thrift stores instead of department stores, cancel Netflix, go to the library instead of buying books every week, etc.

Back to the topic at hand, though. When we write out why we don't have the things we want and then actually focus on overcoming these excuses, we are taking the fault away from them. It's not your kids' fault that you don't have time; it's your fault that you have horrible time management. BOOM. The solution to getting what you want is fixing your time management.

What used to be a problem that you blamed your kids for is now an issue that you can fix with just a few changes in your thought process and your actions.

GAINING CONTROL AS A VETERAN OF WEALTH

As a person who has already had some success, you have probably already accepted the fact that shit happens. But this doesn't mean that you accept that bad things happen and simply stop trying to prevent them. It means that you need to prevent them before they happen because, guess what? They are all within your control. Therefore, you have to proactively search for things to control that will help your business succeed.

The best way to do this is in three steps. The first step is to identify every possible thing that could go wrong with your business (including things that have already gone wrong). Make a list, check it a dozen times, and make sure you are mentally aware of every blunder or screw up that could possibly happen.

The second step is to identify solutions to the problems that are within your scope. This could be as simple as checking your support staff's messages once a week or adding a more explicit terms of services to your website to prevent a future frivolous lawsuit. However, you will not have a solution for some of these problems. This is when we move on to step three.

The third step is identifying people that have done exactly what you want to do and asking them two things. The first is how to fix the current problems that you have already identified. The second is learning about any big issues they ran into that you did not identify. The odds are they will bring up tons of problems that you haven't thought about yet.

You see, a person who has already been in your shoes can tell you what happened while they were there and what happened in the years that followed. Even with the best foresight in the world, you cannot truly predict the future.

People who are a few steps ahead of you in a similar business can save you from lawsuits, website crashes, security leaks, costly errors, and huge pitfalls that typically exist in your business or might exist in your business in the future. By not seeking help, you are leaving your future up to chance. Any of these things could knock you out. But, by receiving support, you are accepting that these issues are your fault (if they do end up happening) and that they are your responsibility to fix, change, and prevent.

CONTROL OF YOUR FUTURE CAN BE SOLELY UP TO YOU

At any time, you can simply decide to pin your downfalls and mishaps on someone else. Socially, you may even be right, and friends and colleagues would agree that, "Oh, if it wasn't for so-and-so, your life would be so awesome." The only problem with this is that this "so-and-so" will never pick up the tab from the damage they have done. They might accept the blame, but they will never truly pay for it.

The only way you can control your future is to take control out of so-and-so's hands and put it all on you—fairly or unfairly. The burden might be heavy, and you might have to beat yourself up quite a bit, but at the end of the day, you will be the one who dodged countless bullets before they were ever even shot.

This pillar is essential, because it allows you to move forward while protecting yourself from needless pitfalls. Protecting ourselves and holding ourselves accountable does not generate money, though. Actions generate money, and this pillar protects us from losing it all in one quick and tragic accident. In order to take the necessary actions, though, we must now learn the lessons that the fifth pillar of wealth can teach us.

THE 5TH PILLAR
ADOPTING AN ABUNDANCE MIND-SET

One of my first businesses after I left the military was (are you ready for this?) . . . a dating coaching business. Yes, I got paid to teach guys how to meet girls at bars and get laid, and yes, this is an actual skill-set that guys can acquire and use. More so, anyone can change who they are socially, which is pretty cool. But that's not the point of this chapter.

I am not going to get into the details of it now, but I used to be a major introvert. And by learning social dynamics and then practicing those dynamics, I taught myself to become extremely competent in social situations. To sum things up, I learned how to drastically stack the odds in my favor in almost any social situation.

With that being said, I can watch any two people interacting and explain what they're doing wrong. I can also give them guidance on how to drastically improve. Over the few years that I practiced and taught how to pick up girls, I was able to learn one of the most important factors in a guy's success. I then noticed that this factor was essential in entrepreneurship and in virtually any aspect of success.

Contrary to popular belief, what you say in social situations has little to do with how much people like you. People's views of you are actually based on how you act. As I stated earlier in this book, how you act (your actions) is also what determines your success in making a bunch of moolah. Now remember, actions are controlled by mind-sets and beliefs. So, in short, a guy's success with women is actually based on his mind-set and core beliefs.

Now, there are many factors that make up your mind-set, but the pillar I am about to cover is one of the most important parts. In fact, without this pillar/factor/belief, a man will always struggle with attracting women, and an entrepreneur will always struggle with making money.

What is this pillar/factor/belief? The answer: The belief in abundance.

Let me explain. Have you ever seen guys trying to pick up girls at a bar and fail miserably? Of course you have. It happens every fifteen seconds in every bar in the world. I would constantly coach men on the subject, and the biggest issue they would have is that they could not get out of their own heads because they lacked abundance. Every girl was treated like she was the last girl on the planet, which in turn made the guys in the situation extremely awkward and nervous. Whenever these guys spoke to a girl, they would continually focus on their own thoughts. They would worry about what she thought of them, what to say next, or if the question they just asked was stupid. All of this thinking basically flat lined the conversation. They would go from being chatty, normal guys to being nervous, annoying, socially awkward weirdos.

To put this in perspective, have you ever had a conversation with someone who was trying way too hard to impress you, wanted something from you, or wanted you to like them a bit too much? This type of conversation does not make anyone feel good.

Seriously, go to a bar and watch men approach women. Most guys simply fall apart in front of a gorgeous girl. Either that or they have to get outrageously drunk to finally gain some confidence. Why does this happen?

It's because they do not believe they have abundance. Before I make my point, let me explain more.

Yes, there are lots of creepy guys at bars. But there is another type of bar guy as well. The confident bar guy.

Have you ever seen a guy who is amazing with women? The next time you are out, I encourage you to try to locate the few guys at the bar who are constantly talking to attractive women. More so, pay attention to the girls who are laughing and smiling right after a man approaches them. You will notice that these men do not seem nervous at all; they seem aloof, nonchalant, and confident. And most of the time, you will notice that they don't seem to really care if the girl likes them or not.

Don't get me wrong, these men would prefer it if the girl they were interested in were also interested in them, but they are simply having fun. They are speaking their minds, being themselves, and just acting like they would with any of their friends. They have no trouble thinking of what to say, because they are not terrified of the girl not liking them back. There are plenty of girls in the world, and if this one doesn't like what he has to say, then she is probably not the right girl. Because of this mind-set, he speaks his mind and enjoys the conversation and interaction. More often than not, girls find this extremely attractive. Women want to talk to men who are calm and happy, not ones who are nervous, awkward, and desperate for approval.

So, how is one guy able to act confidently around women while another guy freezes up? It's simple. The calm and non-chalant guy believes he has abundance. If the girl does not like him, he will find another girl. It's not really a big deal at all. This thought process allows him to be himself and have fun.

On the flip side, the awkward guy becomes nervous because he is terrified of rejection. He believes that one No is the end of the world. This causes him to act super awkward, pushy, needy, or shy, which makes the girl uninterested within thirty seconds of meeting.

The sad part is that all of this comes down to one simple belief: the nervous guy thinks that there is a finite amount of girls in the world, and the calm guy knows that there is an abundance of women in the world. If a guy believes he is good with women and believes that there is an unlimited amount of women that could like him, he is usually *really* successful with them. If a guy believes that he is bad with women and that there is a limited amount of girls that might actually like him, he is usually *really* unsuccessful with them.

The same belief of abundance applies to money and how easily you can make it.

In this chapter, I will explain the nuts and bolts of this pillar like I always do. However, before I get started I want to share with you a universal truth. Money is *repulsed* by people with a scarcity mind-set. People who think that making lots of money is confusing, out of their control, and/or nearly impossible because of their situations (a.k.a. excuses) will always have trouble making more of it . . . just like men who think that getting lots of girls to like them is confusing, out of their control, and/or nearly impossible because of their situations (a.k.a. excuses) will always have trouble getting girls.

The second part of this truth is that people who think in abundance will attract money like flies on shit. These are the people who think that the amount of money they can generate is endless and, if they work hard enough, easy to obtain. People like this might have ups and downs reaching wealth, but money will always find them.

This universal truth is why the rich (usually) get richer and why the poor (usually) stay poor. This is also why poor people who truly believe they can be billionaires usually obtain some level of wealth or at least get out of the poor bracket. If you think about it, it's impossible to think you can become a billionaire without believing that money is abundant.

With that being said, let me break down how lacking the feeling of abundance will paralyze your ability to become wealthy.

Before I get into it, let's go back to the dating analogy to talk about the extremes of this pillar. Let's imagine that you are at a bar full of attractive people. Going home with one of these people represents having a million-dollar business. There are a few types of people you can be. What I want you to do is choose the mind-set analogy that you relate to the most. And, if it's one of the first three, then I want you to learn how to switch your beliefs to the abundance mind-set.

MR. NEVER TAKES RISKS (SUPER SCARCITY MIND-SET)

Let's compare money and dating for people who have the super scarcity mind-set. We'll start with dating first. Having extreme scarcity with dating means that you focus on the girl that you're approaching while thinking that there are no other girls in the world, just like my example a few paragraphs ago.

Having these feelings means you *never* take any risks. You don't want to say anything that could be seen as offensive, because this is your one chance to impress the only girl in the entire world. This causes you to act average—not saying anything horrific, but also not saying anything captivating either. You will not be memorable, and you will not seem any different than the three other guys who approached that girl the same night. After all is said and done, your chance of taking home any girl is almost zero.

If we switch the focus to money, the same results apply. People have a super scarcity mind-set about money *never* do anything that they would consider a risk. They get good grades in high school, go to a decent college, and get safe jobs so they can save money until they die. (As we talked about in an earlier chapter, this is actually a giant negative risk. But no one learns that this typical life is risky, so this is actually how people live if they're afraid of risk.) Because of this, they will probably never be dirt poor, but they will never be rich either. Their lives will be modest, average, and unmemorable, because they see money as a nonrenewable resource and, as such, never take any risks. They have a mental limit as to how much money they can make and how much they can save. They think that they'll end up poor if they take any financial risks, so they simply stay the same for the rest of their lives. But when has playing it safe (a.k.a. doing what everyone else is doing) ever resulted in a remarkable outcome?

Having this one view will keep you poor or, at most, financially average for the rest of your life.

MR. WATCH BUT NOT DO (EXTREME SCARCITY MIND-SET)

While Mr. Never Takes Risks might never do anything he considers to be risky, he is still taking shots. He will go up to a girl and attempt to get her phone number . . . he just rarely succeeds because he puts too much pressure on himself, and only focuses on the negative outcomes. Mr. Watch But Not Do has such a severe scarcity mind-set that he never even attempts anything. This guy doesn't even have the balls to approach a woman at a bar.

This is the guy at the bar who watches everyone else and criticizes them. He laughs at strangers for striking out when he himself never even leaves the bench the whole game. His mind-set is that he could never get a girl, so why even try? The fear of losing is so strong that he cannot take any action.

You all know who this person is when it comes to money. This is the guy who is always poor and still sleeping on a futon at thirty years old with no real desire for a bed. He never sets goals because he thinks money is something that cannot be created at will. He doesn't have X, Y, and Z, so money is just not obtainable.

This is a different type of scarcity mind-set, but it still stops people from ever becoming rich. They don't believe they can be rich, so they never even try. They watch people get rich all the time, but they will stay average (or below average) forever.

MR. BRUTE FORCE (HIGH ABUNDANCE MIND-SET)

This is my favorite type of guy. We all know him and try to avoid him, but he will usually get what he's searching for. This is the guy at the bar who is horrible with women but truly does not care. He knows his skills are lacking and he still gets nervous approaching women, but he will try anything and everything to get laid. His strategy is a simple numbers game. Sure, twenty women in a row might reject him, but eventually one girl will think that his corny pickup lines are "adorable" and agree to go home with him. This guy acts like an idiot and takes crazy risks, such as approaching a group of girls alone or slapping a girl's ass before he even says hello. However, even though he might offend the entire bar with his obnoxious attitude, he rarely goes home alone at the end of the night.

While this guy is horrible with women, he believes he will eventually get one, and eventually he does. His abundance mind-set makes up for his utter lack of social skills. He knows that the worst-case scenario is just rejection. He is not going to die if he fails, and he has unlimited tries.

This guy has the exact same mind-set as the entrepreneurs you see on TV who failed twenty times yet became millionaires on their twenty-first try. In wealth, you only need to "get laid" once. Sam Walton (the creator of Walmart) was one of these people. He had to wait until he was in his sixties to finally "get laid" with his Walmart idea.

While this view of abundance is high risk, if you play a game enough times, you will eventually get good enough and make the right choices needed to win. Just like Mr. Brute Force, you also have unlimited tries. The worst-case scenario is that your business fails and you go bankrupt. At that point, you simply try again by working a crap job while building your next business.

There is no death penalty for failing at business. You just get bad credit and are poor for a while. But guess what? You are already poor! If you can't buy a Ferrari in cash or get on a flight to the Cayman Islands in the next four hours, then I assume you are not as wealthy as you want to be. You might not be in a box, but you're still stuck.

I know all of this may seem extreme, especially for the beginners reading this book. But you must have an extreme mind-set to succeed in this world. If you are not willing to risk it all, then you simply don't want it badly enough. And, as I've mentioned time and time again, if you don't want it badly enough, you will never achieve it.

Long story short, you can see how having an abundance mind-set and believing with all your heart that you will eventually get laid (in business) will, in fact, eventually result in you getting laid. The thing is, just like with dating, you must learn from each failure. You will eventually stop making the same mistakes and increase your chance of success every time you take another shot. And you will eventually turn into the most powerful guy at the "money bar."

MR. LADIES' MAN (EDUCATED ABUNDANCE MIND-SET)

This is the guy at the bar who does not have to try to get girls. He knows he's cool, he has amazing social skills, he's probably pretty good looking, and he is 100 percent confident in who he is. Because of this, when he is at the bar he simply has fun. He talks to everyone around him and meets women just by being himself. Girls are naturally attracted to him because he is having fun and isn't desperate to impress them.

He takes calibrated social risks. He understands people, and he knows that not everyone will like him (because there is not one person on this planet who is universally liked by everybody). He is fine with this fact, and he doesn't let it phase him at all because he is confident in who he is. He is naturally charming, and he also has a lot of knowledge about how humans interact with one another. Because of this, he knows how to guess the outcome of certain actions before he even takes them. There is always a risk, but he understands that the negative outcome would not be severe, and he also knows how to mitigate that risk so it barely even affects him.

This results in Mr. Ladies' Man getting laid more nights than not. He just gets it. He understands that there are millions of women in the world, and he also understands what women like in a man (for a night, at least).

This is the *exact* same thing as being an educated abundance mind-set entrepreneur. Every entrepreneur I know believes that they can make unlimited money and knows that money is limitless. They also understand how money works and essentially what money likes in a man. My goal is to get you to this point by the end of this book.

The point of this chapter is that once you understand all there is to know about money, an abundance mind-set will push you to take the risks needed to make *a lot* of money. I have friends who can almost always predict the stock market, yet they still work behind a desk. Imagine if they took a risk by quitting their jobs and investing in the stock market? They'd have more money than they knew what to do with. But the simple lack of abundance mind-set is what holds them back. (Also, isn't it silly that so many people see change in general as scary? Even if there is a higher chance of succeeding after the change happens?)

IT'S HARD TO HAVE ABUNDANCE WITHOUT ABUNDANCE

Just like with most things in life, it's hard to have a belief without the actions attached to it, which means that it's hard (but not impossible, obviously . . . that's why I wrote this book!) to have an abundance mind-set without actually having abundance. But you need an abundance mind-set to get the abundance in the first place! Because of this mini catch-22, we have to go back to the core and change our beliefs to actually trick our brains into thinking we have abundance right now (which I'll explain in the next section of this chapter).

Remember Mr. Brute Force? Most guys I met while I was a dating coach started out as Mr. Brute force before becoming Mr. Ladies' Man. Mr. Brute Force was experiencing the situations that reinforced the abundance mind-set, even though he did not truly have abundance (yet). At that point, to become Mr. Ladies' Man, all he had to do was calm down a bit and understand how to limit his failures. He had the mind-set but needed to adopt some of the other pillars in this book to become successful at picking up girls.

The challenge, though, is understanding the actions that you must take to obtain this mind-set. Like always, let me spell this out for you.

HOW TO ACHIEVE ABUNDANCE AS A NEWCOMER OF WEALTH

Having an abundance mind-set does not actually have any-thing to do with having money or spending money. You can be extremely poor and still master this mind-set, and having this mind-set will eventually lead you to actions that make you rich. The reason for this is because it is not about having money; it's about knowing there is always a way to make more money.

Let me explain. When you have a finite mind-set, your sole focus is about how to save money wisely and how to spend money wisely. You have a mind-set where you do not believe that money can be generated on command. People who work an eight-to-five job they hate but won't quit are an example of this. Your every thought is about avoiding perceived (negative) risks and saving money. This will naturally stop you from mov-ing forward in a substantial way.

When I was trying to get out of the Air Force and first started in SEO, I didn't have an abundance of money. However, I had spoken with and met many people who were making a killing with Internet marketing. By simply meeting and talking to these people, I adopted the belief that I could be successful in this business, too, because these people were just like me. And if they could do it, so could I.

Because of this, I did not focus on living within my means and sustaining an income. I instead focused on giving myself as much of a chance to make money as possible. I found super cheap rent in a college town that was well below my means and woke up every day with the focus of making money. I did not focus on saving money because the idea of saving (not doing/buying everything you want) contradicts the idea of abundance.

What you need to take away from this story is that my sole focus was on making money because I knew the world had an abundance of it. Because of this, I took actions that lead me to where I am today.

With that being said, the best way to start moving towards an abundance mind-set is to write yourself a mental $1 million check that you will be able to mentally cash once your business becomes successful. Any time you have to decide whether to invest in your business or to save your money, remember that there is $1 million coming your way. That $50 or $1,000 you have to spend on software or educational tools or a freelance website proofreader is going to be laughable when you cash that mental check. Stop worrying about the fifty cents you are saving with a Walmart coupon and start focusing on how to increase your net worth by $10,000 daily.

I'm not saying that you should go buy your girlfriend a new $3,000 handbag because you know you have $1 million coming your way one day. I simply mean do not be afraid to spend the money you need to in order to grow your business . . . and to eat and live, obviously. So, do not spend your money just to spend it, and do not worry about money just to worry about it. Save as much money as you can without worrying and stressing over every penny. Switch your focus from "how to save the money I already have" to "how to make more money today." Also, learn how to spend your money intelligently and believe that more money will come out of it. By solely focusing on conservation, you will never be able to expand.

HOW TO ADOPT ABUNDANCE AS A VETERAN OF WEALTH

The biggest challenge I see after entrepreneurs start making money is that they quickly plateau because they do not know how to spend money wisely. While they have the money, they simply pocket it and try to remain as cheap as possible. But it is incredibly important to remember that there is a difference between spending money and investing it.

While getting things done at the lowest price possible and being smart with our business spending are good things, hoarding money out of fear is extremely damaging for your business (and your mental well-being). I see entrepreneurs who are on the brink of making millions, but they won't hire a staff or spend money on advertising out of fear. You can show them every statistic proving to them that they will make their money back hand over fist, but they still clench every dollar they make like it's the last one they will ever see.

Just like in life, if you do the same thing over and over again in business, nothing will ever change or grow. You can't expect your outcomes to drastically change if your actions don't drastically change first. This is never truer than when it comes to investing in your business. My best advice to you is to identify a few places where you can grow and find a way to mathematically prove to yourself that you will get a return. Find ways to spend your money so you can expand your business, and you will start to see your business grow at an alarming rate.

Many entrepreneurs have an abundance mind-set when they begin, but the second they have something to lose, they revert back into a gold-hoarding cave troll. Don't be one of these entrepreneurs, because your competition will eventually catch up to you, and your ghetto-rigged, low-investment business will soon implode.

Whenever you feel scarcity creeping into your life, start looking for ways to expand. You must keep abundance in your life and keep giving yourself proof that there is abundance. The best ways to prove this to yourself are by expanding your business and by doing anything possible to create more wealth.

ABUNDANCE IS PROGRESS, SCARCITY IS LACK OF PROGRESS

The bold font above this sentence sums it all up. Business can be a minefield at times, but if you never try to cross the minefield because you're too afraid of what might happen, then you never even give yourself a chance to get to the other side.

Traffic fighters focus on hoarding every penny that they make so they can spend it later. Smart entrepreneurs focus on spending every dollar they need to so that they can make ten dollars off of each dollar in the future.

There is unlimited money in the world, and you can take unlimited actions to get it. The only thing that stops these actions is scarcity. You can combat this by adopting the fifth pillar into your life immediately.

THE 6TH PILLAR
FORGETTING "WHAT IF" AND FOCUSING ON "WHAT IS"

I'm going to start off this chapter with a little made-up story. Ben and Roy started working at a car dealership on the same day. Both men were incredibly similar; they had exactly the same education, background, and amount of money in the bank. The only difference between them was that Ben was always thinking about what-ifs and Roy was only focused on the problems right in front of him, a.k.a. what is.

On their first day of work, Ben spent the entire day watching other salesman and reading books on selling. He was terrified that he might mess up and wanted to be able to cover any possible situation before ever even talking to a customer.

Roy, on the other hand, realized that he had only one "problem" (and one thing to focus on), which was getting customers to buy cars. Because of this, he spent his whole first day approaching customers and trying to get sales. He quickly realized that he was a pretty crappy salesman and that customers did not respond to his sales pitch. He went home that night and spent a few hours on Google trying to figure out what he did wrong and how he could fix it.

Both men sold zero cars on their first day.

The next morning, Ben saw something on the news about a car salesman in another town getting sued for selling a defective car. While Ben's boss reassured him that there were no defective cars on their lot, Ben was still worried that he might get sued one day for the same issue. He was so focused on this news story that he spent his whole second day learning about defective cars and inspecting every car in his area for defects.

On the other side of the lot, Roy kept working at his only problem, selling cars. In his research the night before, he learned a trick to change his sales pitch. This resulted in him selling one car that morning. He almost sold two other cars, but lost the customers in negotiation. Roy then realized his new problem was negotiating. After work, he went home, sat on his computer, and focused on learning how to negotiate.

Ben sold zero cars and Roy sold one car on their second day.

On the third day, Ben talked to Roy, and Roy mentioned that negotiating gave him trouble. Ben, who at this point had still not talked to a single customer, decided that he needed to learn how to negotiate before taking any action. He spent the whole day walking around the lot asking other sales people how to negotiate.

Roy, on the other hand, sold four cars because of his great sales pitch and because he learned that people were more likely to buy a car if he gave them a discount on leather seats during negotiation.

Ben sold zero cars and Roy sold four cars on their third day.

The next day, a customer who bought a car the previous day came in angry with Roy because Roy had been incorrect about some of the car's details since he was in such rush to sell cars. Roy apologized and refunded the customer. Ben saw this and was scared that it would happen to him, so he spent all day memorizing all the details for all the cars in the lot.

While Ben was memorizing car details, Roy fixed the issue, then repeated the same process he used the day before. Because of this, he sold six cars.

Ben sold zero cars and Roy sold six cars on their fourth day.

On the fifth day, both car salesmen got called into the owner's office. At this point, even though Roy had made some mistakes, he sold a total of eleven cars. He also knew how to fix his mistakes, since he had dealt with them firsthand. Ben, on the other hand, had made zero mistakes but had also sold zero cars. He learned how to fix a ton of hypothetical problems, but had no real-world experience with the mistakes or with the potential/necessary fixes.

Their boss gave Roy a bonus check and thanked him for all the new sales. He also said that Roy was moving toward being the best salesman the dealership had ever had. Then the boss turned to Ben and said, "Ben, we need people who can get sales. Why have you not sold a single car this week?"

Ben replied, "I know I haven't sold any cars, but I wanted to prepare first so that I don't make any mistakes with my customers. I saw other people's problems with angry customers, forgetting car details, and lawsuits, and I wanted to make sure I could prevent them before they happen."

The boss then replied with, "All these issues you have brought up are nothing to worry about. We have never been sued for defective cars, and everyone knows that customers will come in angry sometimes. Your focus should not be potential issues; your focus should be whatever is right in front of you. Right now, it is selling cars. If you cannot sell a car today, then we will have to let you go."

For the rest of the day, Ben tried to sell a car, but he ran into the real problems that Roy had on his first day: he didn't have a sales pitch. This meant that he couldn't solve his most immediate issue, which was just getting a damn sale.

By the end of the day, Ben was fired for underperforming. Roy, on the other hand, sold another seven cars. Within a month, Roy was the best-selling car salesman at the dealership because, every day, he focused on the problems in front of him and then he figured out how to solve them. By the end of the month, he had the most lethal sales pitch on the car lot. He made some big mistakes in that time, but by making those mistakes, he learned how to fix them.

Why did Ben fail while Roy succeeded, even though they had identical backgrounds and the same incentives? It's fairly simple and comes down to one thing: Roy took action and dealt with problems when they became problems while Ben took very little action and focused solely on hypothetical problems. He was locked in "perfection paralysis," and because of this, he was never able to move forward or succeed like Roy did.

This is what the sixth pillar is all about. In order to reach your goals, you have to take a certain number of steps (actions) to get there. By taking these steps, you will naturally run into problems. But, as we all know by now, the best way to learn is to experience something yourself. There is no possible way you can accurately predict and prevent every potential problem. And, even if you could, you wouldn't be able to truly understand the problem unless you experienced the problem. For example, imagine that someone taught you how to fix a toaster, but you've never even looked at a toaster before. Situations are completely different from an outside perspective compared to when you're facing them head on.

In fact, once you start taking your steps, it is unlikely that the things you thought would be problems will actually arise, and other situations you never even considered may come to bite you in the ass. The overall point is that planning for every potential problem before you take action will not help you succeed. It will either lengthen the time it takes you to reach your goal, or you'll never reach your goal at all, similar to Ben in the above example. If you want to advance in your field or your business, you must stop thinking about it and stop planning it, and just take action.

Over the past several years, I have worked directly and indirectly with literally thousands of people who are trying to build an online business. Whether I met these people through direct coaching or via large-group coaching on online education platforms, I have always seen an obvious trend. The people who take reckless action are usually the ones who succeed. The people who think too much while trying to get everything perfect on the first try are usually the ones who never succeed. Why?

They never move forward because they cannot get it perfect, and eventually quit out of frustration.

This is why this pillar is so important. In the fourth pillar, I mentioned to you that you must take responsibility for everything that happens to you and do your best to predict situations. And, like every pillar, it is about having a balance between everything. Yes, you must take complete control of your situation, but you also must take the actions or steps needed to get to your goal. If you do not, you will get locked in perfection paralysis.

Perfection paralysis is when you are so focused or worried about getting things right that you never make a move (just like Ben). I want you to imagine a hockey player who is trying to master shooting the puck. He could read every book, watch every video, and join the local hockey club. However, in order for him to make any progress, he has to shoot the damn puck. There are 1,001 things that could go wrong once he shoots, but the only real problem he has at the moment is that he hasn't even taken a shot (taken a chance, tried, attempted, etc.).

Once he takes a shot, problems will naturally spring up. And when a problem appears, he will have a chance to learn from it and correct it. Then, when more problems arise, he will fix those too. Focusing on problems that haven't happened will increase your stress and possibly even deter you from reaching your goal at all. How many times have you thought of a business but never even started because you thought of all the problems that could arise? "What if we go bankrupt?" "What if no one buys my software?" "What if some celebrity buys my training product and complains about it all over the Internet?"

By focusing on problems when they happen (not before, not after), you will have more time, energy, and mental space to see the situation for what it really is versus what could potentially happen. Back to the hockey analogy, this is why a guy who has taken two thousand shots with little training will always do better than a guy with ten years of training who has never gotten on the ice. Even better, the guy with two thousand shots will know exactly when he needs training and what he needs to practice.

Let me give you a personal example.

One of my first main businesses was teaching people how to get clients for their Search Engine Optimization (SEO) businesses. This is one of the most profitable and easiest businesses to start, in my opinion.

Now, in my training I tell people the most important thing to learn is selling, and the best way to learn how to sell is to get experience selling. Yes, these people need to become efficient at providing the service they are selling. However, no matter how good they become at SEO, they will not get paid until they learn how to sell their SEO services and get their first client. Got it?

One of the biggest challenges I would see is perfection paralysis. I would see people spend months learning SEO and asking tons of questions about selling, yet they would never pick up the phone to sell. They would constantly ask super specific questions about providing the service, legal matters, and every possible problem you could ever imagine. In the end, many would not make money because they ignored my initial advice of sell, sell, sell.

I want to tell you about a person who did take my advice, though. His name is Kotton Grammer. He came into my group unemployed and nearly broke. He once asked me an irrelevant and improbable what-if question on a live webinar, and my response was, "That will probably never happen, so don't think about it. Focus on the problem you currently have. Your only problem right now is getting clients, so go get clients."

Kotton took this to heart and began to solely focus on getting clients, even though he was still nervous about providing the service. After about three months of complete focus, Kotton got his first client.

At this point, Kotton's new problem was providing the service. He focused on that problem, and it only took him about a week to get the client results. (He already had the confidence, brainpower, and background knowledge to master this particular service, which is why he went in that direction in the first place.)

After this sale, Kotton became a selling machine. He got another client, and another, and another. He completely mastered the only immediate problem he had, which was "selling his services and getting clients." Within one year, Kotton went from being broke and unemployed to making over $100,000 in profit a month selling SEO services to large companies.

Fast-forward another year, and Kotton was making well over $400,000 a month in profit by selling SEO services. He also has become one of the greatest SEO salespeople (if not the greatest) of all time. Yes, this is a true story. And no, I am not exaggerating.

How the hell did he do this? He did it by constantly taking shots and fixing the problems he had in front of him. Instead of focusing on the 1,001 things that could go wrong, he focused on his one current problem. First, it was getting clients. After he got his first client, he *then* focused on his next problem: providing the service. By solely focusing on the problem at hand, he solved each one and quickly mastered them all.

At some point, you have to stop thinking about what-ifs and focus on what is. Forward motion is the name of the game, and wondering about what might happen does not help you win. Obsessing over the what-ifs keeps you anxious, stressed, and in your quiet little comfort zone of learning. Action is the only thing that moves you forward and the only thing that results in true understanding.

However, since birth we are taught to think in terms of "what if." We are led to believe that failure is final and mistakes are unacceptable. When we think of doing anything, we think, "What if this is not right?" and, "What if I can't do that?" These thoughts are natural because of what our culture teaches us, but if we let these negative and worrisome beliefs control us we will end up like Ben, the fired car salesman.

In order to reach our goals, we have to rearrange in our heads how we look at failures, mistakes, and messing up. Here's how.

HURRY UP AND GET IT WRONG

As you saw in the car salesmen story, getting it wrong is not the most damaging thing you can do in wealth creation. The single worst thing you can do when trying to reach your goals is not doing anything at all. In fact, in most cases getting it wrong at the start can be far more beneficial than getting it right in the long term. Let me explain.

Most people think that true education and skill are taught by action. While this is true, the best way to learn is not just by taking action, but by making mistakes. You can read a book on coding, but you won't become an expert until you actually start writing code. More so, you won't learn the most important lessons of coding until your first application explodes in your face.

Here's another hockey example for you guys. You can watch people play hockey all day long while you sit on the bench, but you won't start making progress until you get on the ice. On top of that, you won't become an expert until you embarrass yourself and get yelled at on the ice by your coach. Why? Because in order for a human being to learn, they must directly experience what is right and what is wrong. You can't experience the right or wrong way to do something until you do it all yourself!

Earlier in this book I mentioned how overlooking a small detail in a payment processor (remember when my employee forgot to check a specific account?) cost me about $20,000. Over my career, mistakes like this have happened many times. I have lost my butt in advertising. I have had sales pages crash with thousands of customers visiting them. I once spoke live for two hours to a crowd online of a thousand people, and once I got to the pitch part of my speech, I realized that I didn't have a way to accept credit card payments for our software. This one mistake probably cost me $40,000. But guess what? Since then,

I have never started an online event without personally testing our checkout process.

Long story short, there have been times when I have *really* gotten it wrong. However, because of these mistakes, I have learned lessons that most people will never learn. I have also been able to make my business three or four times more profitable in the process. Essentially, my business is built upon lessons that were born from mistakes, and most other successful businesses are the exact same way.

Before I get to my point, I am not saying that you shouldn't try to mitigate mistakes. What I am saying is that you can't let the fear of messing up stop you from taking action. Imagine if I had let the fear of messing up stop me from working on these projects. Sure, the mistake would have never happened and I could have kept my entrepreneur report card blemish-free. However, the success (and money) that these mistakes lead to never would have happened either.

In short, action will almost always lead to mistakes. But, without taking action, you'll never reach success. Therefore, there is very little chance of reaching success without making mistakes.

The biggest lesson I am trying to pound into your heads is that the sooner you make your mistakes, the sooner you will hit your success. When you start any business in which you are not experienced, there is going to be a period of time where it just flat-out sucks. Everything will go wrong, and you will make a lot of gut-wrenching mistakes. These mistakes might knock you down, make you feel stupid, or deter you from continuing, but you have to try your best to fight those negative thoughts. What you must do is take so much action that you learn from these mistakes and get through them as fast as possible.

From now on, you must believe that the definition of a mistake is, "A lesson that will make you money in the future," instead of the traffic fighter definition of, "A reason not to take action."

WHAT IF YOU ARE POOR FOR THE REST OF YOUR LIFE?

Now that you understand that what-ifs are success stoppers, I am here to teach you how to get rid of your what-if mind-set and adopt a what-is mind-set.

Every time you are presented with an action-stopping what-if, you need to ask yourself these what-ifs instead:

- What if I do not take action on my goal?
- What if I am poor for the rest of my life?
- What if I fail to reach any of my goals?
- What if I have to work at this job that I hate for the next thirty years?
- What if I cannot provide for my family?
- What if I end up regretting all of this on my deathbed?

Go ahead, try it. Think about a few of the big what-ifs that are stopping you from starting a business or trying to get rich. Write them down if you have to. Then ask yourself the what-ifs above. Sometimes simply writing your current what-ifs next to the above what-ifs will start to switch your train of thought. If it doesn't, then write down the answers to all of the what-ifs. For example:

Current what-if: What if my first business fails?

The answer: I'll lose some money and feel like I have wasted my time.

More important what-if: What if I fail to reach any of my goals?

The answer: I will be disappointed in myself, I'll have to pinch pennies until I die, and I will never be able to pay for my three kids to go to college.

Think about it. Is the idea of possibly failing at your new business more terrifying than the idea of living paycheck to paycheck for the rest of your life?

Is the fact that you might lose a client because you messed up scarier than looking back at your life when you're older and regretting not even trying?

Is the thought that you might struggle to succeed for a few years worse than working ten-hour days at a traffic fighter job for the next thirty or forty years of your life?

I can tell you right now that the fear of looking back on my life and not doing something important outweighs any what-if I have today. Because of this, I am not weighed down by the little doubts that creep into my life.

Sometimes, the only way to conquer one fear is to motivate yourself with a bigger fear. You must find things that are utterly unacceptable and use them to push you past the gripes you have today. However, this is not always enough.

Most of the time, simply wanting to be rich will not be enough to push you past your what-ifs. You have to understand that, as humans, we are much more motivated by avoiding pain than we are by achieving gain. As I mentioned earlier in this book, if your current situation is tolerable, then you probably aren't going to have a strong motivation to get out of it. This is why many people want to be rich but never become rich because of their what-ifs.

What you must do is find the emotionally painful what-ifs that can trigger you to completely ignore your temporary, whiny what-ifs.

Think about it. For me, I wanted to become successful because I was bullied as a child and my job was unbearably bad. Everyone in my neighborhood tried to make me feel stupid and inferior. Instead of actually making me feel inferior, these bullies pushed me to be superior. I wanted to show everyone that I was not only as smart as them but actually smarter and more determined than they were. I wanted to be successful so I could shove it in their faces. On top of that, I dreaded the thought of staying at my current, horrible job in the military (which I already spoke about in the first chapter). These combined factors caused me a ton of emotional stress.

At that point, my what-ifs were: "What if I am seen as a failure my whole life?" and, "What if I have to work at this job for the rest of my life?" These what-ifs may seem superficial or downright silly to you, but they pissed me off enough to make me *have* to become successful.

The sole desire to become rich will never get you past your what-ifs. Your entrepreneurial what-ifs would result in pain if you fail, whereas your current life circumstances do not actually cause you pain. Possible pain versus current comfort won't push you to work hard and succeed. You must find a deeper current agony to make a change.

So, take a moment and think about the thing (or multiple things) that is or would be unbearable if you never changed your lifestyle and if you stayed at your current job with your current income and house and car and hobbies and daily schedule. Maybe it's being a failure in the eyes of others. Maybe it's your current crappy job. Maybe it's living a mediocre life. Maybe it's living paycheck to paycheck. Maybe it's never being able to pay off your house. Whatever it is, identify it. Then, whenever you confront yourself with pointless entrepreneurial what-ifs, replace them with the truly painful what-ifs you have just identified.

As always, the next steps are a bit more detailed and are based on where you are in your entrepreneurial life.

Let's get into them.

HANDLING WHAT-IFS AS A BEGINNER

What-ifs are essentially a lethal injection for beginners in wealth generation. From the second we are born, we are taught to go down the safe route. Because of this, we "what if" any idea that comes our way. On top of that, we are trained to not move forward until our what-ifs are solved.

As you have (hopefully) learned in this book, society's safe route isn't too safe, and lack of action equals being poor. Therefore, if you're a beginner at wealth generation you must surpass this.

As I previously mentioned, I have worked with many beginners via large, mass business coaching groups. I no longer do this, and here's why: I could give an entire completed business plan to beginners, and instead of taking action, they will create what-ifs. Even worse, they will not move forward until someone solves these what-ifs for them. After the what-ifs are solved, you'd think they could finally start taking action, right? Nope, they go on to create more what-ifs. It drives me up a damn wall.

I will literally see people ask a question and not take a single step forward with their business until it is answered, even if it takes weeks to get answered. They will then ask another question as soon as their first one is resolved, which results in more waiting. Because of all of their what-ifs and all of this waiting, they end up taking about two steps out of the twenty thousand needed to reach their goal . . . over the span of an entire month.

In short, most beginners never focus on the what-is that is right in front of them. They don't focus on the immediate actions they need to do now because they are too busy focusing on the what-ifs in the future.

This is why coaching beginners is usually a fruitless endeavor. No tactic or strategy in the world is going to work if you are stopping every ten seconds to focus on a what-if.

So, as a beginner, you must develop a system to keep you on track with your goal. You must also realize that you don't have to do everything perfect the first time to eventually succeed.

What you must first do is recognize your "absolute simple problem." This is the problem that is stopping you from getting rich, and you need to identify it down to the simplest and easiest describable form. By doing this, it makes finding the solutions quite easy.

For example, if you are starting a business where you need clients (which is all businesses, isn't it?), you might be wondering how to get started. Do you learn selling, do you master providing the service, do you buy pretty business cards . . . where the heck do you start?

You want to start at your biggest problem: getting paid. (I know we already went over this, but I'm going to repeat myself, like always, because I need you guys to truly understand this concept.)

Now, how do you get paid? You get a client! The end. Your biggest issue is getting a client, and your only issue is getting a client to buy your product or service. Everything you *do* should be focused around this one outcome. Everything you *learn* should be focused around this one outcome.

Instead of focusing on the what-if problems in the future that may never become a reality, you instead must focus on your current reality. You must focus on what-is. Your current what-is is you need to get paid. Period. You must solve this problem before ever wondering about what-ifs.

Next, lay out the one thing you need to learn to do this. In this situation, it would be that you need to learn how to sell. Then, after that, identify three immediate actions you can start doing *right now* that can result in getting a client.

These could be:

1. Cold calling businesses.
2. Emailing businesses.
3. Attending business networking events.

Then, you put all of this in an action paragraph.

"My only issue is getting a client. I need to learn selling and only selling. I need to be cold calling businesses, e-mailing businesses, and attending business events at every possible opportunity I have."

That's it. By doing this, there is very little room for what-ifs, because your focus is on the task at hand. If a what-if does creep into the equation, simply repeat your action paragraph to yourself and stick to it. Even if you mess up, sticking to the statement will eventually result in some form of success.

You will never be able to fully rid yourself of what-ifs. However, you can always have an answer for them that drastically lowers the amount of time you spend thinking about them and increases the time you spend taking action to reach your goal.

HANDLING WHAT-IFS AS A VETERAN

As a person who has already made money as an entrepreneur, you probably think that you are above the problem of what-ifs. But, since I know that you're reading this book because you want to make more money, I am sorry to say that the problem of what-ifs absolutely does apply to you. In fact, you are probably more debilitated by them than a beginner. It's just a different kind of what-if that affects you.

More often than not, entrepreneurs will plateau at some point. This happens when they have enough money to live comfortably and don't feel the need to work harder. That's when growing and becoming more successful becomes difficult. They plateau because they stop taking drastic actions, and they stop taking drastic actions because a new and much scarier what-if has entered their life:

"What if I lose what I just spent the last three, five, ten, or twenty years growing?"

When a person is starting out, they are generally close to rock bottom, so failing is not the worst thing in the world; they can't actually lose that much. However, once they have a decent amount of money and success, losing that money and success is the scariest thing in the world.

Think of it this way: Imagine you're trying to jump from one roof of a building to a neighboring roof ten feet away from it like they do on TV sometimes. If the roofs are only one story high, jumping will be scary because it's something you've never done before, but it won't be the scariest thing you'll ever do in your life, and the negative risk isn't that severe. But, if the roofs are fifteen stories high, attempting that jump will be moderately terrifying. You can make it, sure, but the negative risk is much higher, and you have much more to lose if you fail to succeed.

Once we have a moderate level of success or are comfortable in our lives, our fear of failure (that what-if) is paralyzing. How do we overcome it?

You might have heard that after Elon Musk sold PayPal, he immediately reinvested *all* of his money into new crazy ventures like SpaceX and Tesla. Elon was not only unaffected by this what-if of investing, but he blew right past it like a raging lunatic on PCP. To him, growth and moving forward outweighed any stupid what-if that may have popped into his head.

With that being said, while I do not advise being as reckless as Elon, his ability to shrug off the "What if I lose it all?" question is remarkable. How did he do this? At a net worth in the billions-of-dollars range, he could have just sat on the cash and been incredibly rich for life. Instead, he opted to risk losing everything. How . . . and why?

Because these investments were his goals and the thought of not reaching his goals was far more painful than losing it all. In order to push ourselves forward, we have to think the same way.

Each entrepreneur is different, and every one of us has different goals. What you have to do is identify your ultimate goal and ask yourself if you can live with yourself if you don't reach this goal. More importantly, you have to find every pain point that comes from not reaching this goal.

I don't know you or what drives you, so what you must do is identify why you want to make more money. Like we talked about earlier, write down reasons that will decrease or eliminate your pain, not reasons that will increase your pleasure (because the promise of decreased pain makes people work harder than the promise of increased pleasure).

The only way you are going to get past the fear of failure is if you have a greater fear of not succeeding. You have to have something that you simply cannot accept living without. If you don't, it is going to be very hard to move forward.

Once you have this list of pains, you need to refer to it often and repeat your goals to yourself as much as possible. You have to stop yourself from becoming comfortable, or you will eventually become so comfortable that you're completely stuck.

THE ONLY DAY ALL YOUR WHAT-IFS ARE ANSWERED IS THE DAY YOU DIE

Sadly, we will never have all of our what-ifs answered in our lifetime, either because we are too ashamed to admit them or because we can't think deeply enough. All the people on their deathbeds know the answers to the big questions that held them back their entire lives.

"What will happen if I don't start my own business? *This.*"

"What will happen if I am poor my whole life? *This.*"

"What will happen if I work my whole life for someone else? *This.*"

More importantly, they are hit with an even more painful question: "What could have happened?" The sad part is that they will never know. It's too late.

Right now, as you read this book, there are a lot of what-ifs in front of you. This is an answer you will only find by taking action. You have to get past the what-ifs that will be answered when it's too late to pursue "what could have happened."

Every successful person I know is plagued by what-ifs just like every unsuccessful person I know. The only difference is that the successful people chose to focus on the what-ifs I listed a few pages ago ("What if I never reach my goals?" etc.) because not answering those is far more painful than the consequences of your fear-based what-ifs. Then, they focus on solving the immediate what-is problems in their life one at a time. By always focusing and solving what-is issues, you are always moving forward, which is the opposite of what happens if you focus on negative what-ifs.

They have accepted the fact that life is in their control and that anything can happen. They also focus on the what-is because that is all there is. They believe their life is a lump of wet clay, and the only way to see the future is to mold it yourself. This leads us to our next pillar.

THE 7TH PILLAR
MAPPING OUT ACTIONS THAT ACHIEVE GOALS

If you do a little bit of research on companies such as Amazon or Facebook, you will notice that they took an extremely long time to become profitable. In fact, Amazon did not reap a profit for almost twenty years. Even crazier, Twitter and Snapchat are worth billions, yet still haven't turned even a dollar in profit.

Confusing, right? How can popular companies be worth so much money without being profitable? Because they are moving in the direction of global domination and will be massively profitable because of the amount of leverage they are gaining. These companies are perfect examples of the seventh pillar mind-set.

The richer a person (or company) is, the better they are at creating and following through on their goals. More importantly, the better they are at mapping out how to reach these goals and understanding what these goals mean for their future.

On the flip side, if you look at someone with low income, they usually have extremely short-term goals, small goals that they don't make much effort to achieve (or make excuses for), or large goals without any mapped out way to reach them. So many people want to become best-selling authors but have no idea how to get a book published. Countless people want to start their own brick-and-mortar businesses but are clueless about how to choose the right part of town for their store.

These facts usually cause the person to forget about their goal completely (or give up) because they feel too overwhelmed with confusing choices. Self-publishing or traditional publishing? Downtown or suburbs? Since they don't know how to plan the goal, they never give themselves a chance to actually reach the goal. But the truth is, creating a plan to reach your goal is actually more important than the goal itself.

Constructing a plan, an action plan, is actually quite easy. All you have to do is write out every step it will take for you to reach your goal. But before you can write out these action steps, there is one more thing you need to understand: you must define your goal first. You must know exactly what your goal entails and what it means for your entire life. Anyone can say, "I want this" or, "I want to become that," but very few people can define what their goal truly means in terms of exactly what they want, what it looks like, and what it feels like as a finished product or met goal.

For example, there are quite a few people who want to build massive skyscrapers in New York City. Donald Trump wanted this too, but instead of simply wanting it, he defined it, and then he created action steps to actually get a building built. When he was first envisioning one of his initial projects, the Grand Hyatt in NYC, he did two things:

1. He defined his goal. He wanted this building to look a certain way, be designed a certain way, and be placed in a certain part of the city. He wanted to attract a certain kind of customer and have a certain kind of image, and he knew how much money he was willing to spend on the construction of the building.

2. He mapped out a way to get there. He knew exactly who he needed to hire, the laws he needed to know, and virtually every small detail that needed to happen to get the hotel completed within his budget.

Years before the hotel ever existed, Donald Trump had already defined his goal and figured out action steps to reach his goal. And guess what? Those thoughts and ideas helped him to reach his goal of creating a beautiful building.

HOW TRAFFIC FIGHTERS PLAN (AND FAIL TO ACHIEVE) THEIR GOALS

If you look at any city highway at 8:00 a.m. (such as the ones I refer to so fondly in the first chapter), you will see tens of thousands of people with big goals. Goals of fame and fortune, goals of becoming a professional chef or a TV news anchor, goals of making millions and buying houses for everyone they know. All of them are just waiting for that right moment to open their business and live life on their own terms.

So why is it that so few of these people ever reach their goals? It's because they know nothing about the details or how to achieve them. All they see is the "success event." The success event is the moment they've made it and have tons of money, thus earning the "good life." But that's as specific as they will get. They think, "I'll have so much money, and I won't have to work at this crappy job anymore." That's it. However, if you ask them any details about that moment or how they could get there, they are clueless.

"How much money will you be making? What will you be known for? How long will it take? Who would be your ideal customer? What will your product be? How many customers do you need to reach your monetary goal? Who needs to support you to reach your main goal?" It's all one giant question mark.

This is why becoming successful is almost viewed as winning the lottery in our society. People only notice the success event. This is why so many people are jealous of the rich and famous. They don't see all the hard work, dedication, and determination that was put into their stardom; they just assume their success happened overnight or that these people got lucky (which I can assure you is not true). Successful people's goals were met because they defined these goals, created action plans, and took small steps to achieve them.

Since I assume most of you reading this book are traffic fighters or very recently got out of the traffic fighter life, you are going to have to totally reengineer how you define and map out your goals.

HOW MULTIMILLIONAIRES PLAN THEIR GOALS

Very few multimillionaires make their money in a single event. Yes, there are buyouts that result in hundreds of millions of dollars made in a day (these are the people who become "overnight successes"), but these buyouts are usually the result of hundreds of tiny events (or steps) over many months or years. Okay, sure—there is the small minority of millionaires that struck oil and won the business lottery. But you cannot rely on this. For all intents and purposes, you must plan your success.

What you must realize is that the big event is a result of many smaller actions coming together. Those actions are built upon hundreds of daily microactions. For example, a man selling his software company for $100 million is not the result of him selling his business. It is the result of him coming up with the idea, spending six months coding the software, hiring the right staff, buying the right advertising, and dozens of other small things. In order to get to the main event, it's important to identify the event you want (your goal) but even more so to identify the hundreds of little things, because those are what actually make up the event.

The first thing multimillionaires do is set big goals. For example, one of my goals is to have a software company that makes over $100 million a year in sales. After I made that goal, I broke it down into hundreds of smaller goals that are definable and attainable. I broke down exactly how many customers we would need, how we would get those customers, and the sales funnels we would need to convert them. I then broke those steps down even further, but we'll get to that.

I want you to be able to do the exact same thing. In order to become rich, you are going to need a way to get there. So now let's go over defining and mapping out your goals.

Step 1: What Is Your Big Goal?

More than likely, if you are new to the idea of wealth creation, you cannot clearly define your big goal. Most people think, "I want a software company," or, "I'd like to make $1 million a year," or, "I want to travel the world with my family and have enough income so I don't have to worry about money," but these are not specific enough.

At a bare minimum, you must have an income goal as well as a defined way to get there (meaning how you are going to achieve the monetary goal, whether it be creating software, writing self-help books, creating video training programs, etc.). But the easiest way to do this is to start at the absolute base of why people want to make money: lifestyle.

I want you to get superficial for a moment and think about all the things you want right now: the cars, the houses, the vacations, the expensive schooling for your children, etc. We are going to turn these answers into an exercise to make you realize your specific big goals and then break them down from there.

It can be extremely beneficial to deeply envision these lifestyle goals. For example, almost three years ago, I envisioned myself owning a large house in uptown Dallas with a Ferrari and a hot tub overlooking the city. Today, I have all of those things, and having this clear-cut goal deeply ingrained in my head (along with my action steps) has helped me to get there.

However, I want to stay away from too much mental masturbation in this book and get down to a purely results-driven mentality. Take some time right now to write down all the things you want in your life that require money. Be specific. Don't just write down "I want a house." Write down the style, size, location, etc.

(To make this exercise simpler for right now, I would suggest not including incredibly grand desires, such as owning a private jet or buying a sports team, or things such as savings and investments. Once you understand the exercise, feel free to include these things. But for now, adding such large desires will complicate the exercise, and I want you to learn it in a simple manner.)

In the space provided, write down everything you want, and remember to be specific.

EVERYTHING YOU WANT

_____

_____

_____

_____

_____

Now I want you to go online and figure out the exact price for each of the things you want. (Just do a Google search on "five-bedroom brick house in Charleston price" or "1960 Jaguar price." Then find the one you want the most and write down the cost.) Then calculate how much money you'd need to acquire all these things and achieve the lifestyle you want. I'm serious; go and do that right now. I can wait.

Are you done? Great. You now have loosely defined how much money you actually need to reach your goal. (I say "loosely" because I know you forgot a few things such as renting a lodge every winter to go skiing with your family or taking flying lessons.) This is a huge step for you because, well, how are you supposed to plan your desired lifestyle if you don't even know what it will cost?

Now let's imagine that you need $5 million to buy every single thing you've ever wanted. The next question is, "How are you going to generate $5 million?" Will it be from publishing a book series? Opening a restaurant? Starting a software company, a real estate firm, or a protein supplement company? Starring in some porn movies? (Kidding!)

Write down whatever your gut tells you. If you don't know yet, then you immediately know what you need to define next in your dream. You must figure out *how* you are going to make money. This is problem no. 1 (like we talked about in the sixth pillar). For now, to complete this exercise, just imagine something you would enjoy. That could be anything from cooking (cookbook series, cooking lessons, cooking tutorials online, etc.) to writing (books, plays, comic books, scripts, speeches for the president, etc.) to playing video games (tournaments, YouTube videos, etc.).

For this exercise, let's say you chose to create a supplement company. Now you need to define what you are going to sell, how much you are going to sell it for, and who your target market is. Yes, this will take research. But don't do that research now; just write down a guesstimate and keep reading so you understand what you'll need to do. Then, when you're done reading this book, go back, reread this chapter, and follow all the steps in order.

Let's say we decided to sell specialty protein powder at $47 a bottle to crossfitters. With these guidelines, we now can actually define our big goal:

"Our big goal is to make $5 million to achieve the lifestyle we want (then list everything you want). In order to do that, we will create a supplement company that sells protein powder at $47 a bottle targeting crossfitters. In order to reach $5 million, we will need to sell 106,383 bottles of protein powder."

Are there other factors that go into this? YES! But we have just defined our big goal and how we will achieve it with a business. That is a huge first step! But, in the sentence above, we are missing *a lot* of information and steps that are necessary for selling 106,383 bottles of protein. This is what step 2 of this exercise is about.

STEP 2: WHAT ARE FIVE SMALLER GOALS YOU MUST ACHIEVE TO REACH YOUR BIG GOAL?

One does not simply just wake up and generate $5 million worth of sales by selling over a hundred thousand bottles of protein powder. There are many, many smaller goals (not small goals, just smaller than your big goal) we need to meet that will allow us to reach our big goal. And, in order to make this a reality, we must define those smaller goals. What I want you to do is look at your proposed business and try your best to think up the five biggest factors that would go into generating your income goal. (Once again, read this whole book first and then come back and complete this exercise so you have all the knowledge you need in order to do it correctly.)

Here are five goals we could have for the protein powder example. (For this first exercise, I suggest having a minimum of three goals and a maximum of five goals. Preferably, these goals would be in chronological order, but getting them written down is the most important part.)

1. Develop the protein powder formula and product.
2. Create a system or platform to sell the product.
3. Find methods of advertising that can attract over a hundred thousand sales.
4. Craft an iconic brand.
5. Sell the protein powder in major stores.

Yes, these are sizable goals. But when we look at them one at a time, it makes our one big goal far more manageable.

What's amazing about this is that we are no longer just thinking, "I want $5 million, cool cars, and a protein powder company." We are instead thinking, "How can I develop a protein powder?" or "How can I advertise this protein powder to make over a hundred thousand sales?" We are actually thinking about achievable goals that are solvable and within our reach.

Step 3: Break Down Each of These Five Goals into Even Smaller Tasks.

Now that we have these five smaller goals listed, we can finally ask questions that we can actually answer.

This right here is why this process is so important. If you think about creating a protein powder company, your brain can go a mile a minute with thoughts and ideas, and you will become overwhelmed very quickly. It's simply too large of a goal to reach on its own. But once you have an action plan and smaller goals listed out, you realize that your big goal is attainable if you take the right steps.

Let's look at "small goal" no. 1: Develop the protein powder formula and product. How can we do this? We simply turn this goal into a list of actions and smaller goals.

(Also note that I personally have developed a protein powder that I will start selling as soon as I am ready to launch the company. I currently have other priorities in my business, so this one has gone on the back burner temporarily. Below, I have listed my exact steps to reach my big goal.)

Step 1: Find out how to develop protein powder in the first place.
How can we do this?

1. Do some Internet research on the subject.
2. Ask people who have done it.
3. Call some protein powder manufacturers and ask them how to get what I need developed.

After we accomplish these steps, we now know how to develop protein powder. All we need to do is some moderate Internet and in-person research and then call manufacturers and tell them what we want created.

Step 2: Identify what crossfitters are looking for in protein powders.
How can we do this?

1. Ask your crossfit friends what they look for in a protein powder.

2. Ask questions on crossfit Facebook pages, forums, and other websites.
3. Attend some events and see what protein powders are getting a crowd.

Boom. We now know that crossfitters are looking for low-carb protein powders.

Step 3: Find out the costs and hire a manufacturer.
How can we do this?
1. Do some more Internet research.
2. Call multiple manufacturers and get a quote.
3. Ask people who have done it before for tips and advice.

Okay, it's going to cost $10,000 to have someone develop the formula and $30,000 to order the 1,500 bottles of it.

Step 4: Come up with $40,000.
How can we do this?
1. Contact investors.
2. Take out a loan.
3. Invest your savings.

Figure out which option works best for you, and boom. The end. While this business does have a significant startup cost, what I want you to look at is how I broke down one of my five big goals and laid out the exact steps I needed to take to achieve it.

Let's imagine I did this for every single one of my five goals. I would end up with a very clear path that I'd need to follow to reach my ultimate goal of $5 million. Instead of having one big lofty goal with no definition, I have a specific and easy-to-follow recipe. This recipe not only makes the actions more manageable but also makes it much more likely that I will start working towards this goal and actually achieve it.

Let's look at the even bigger picture, though. Before this exercise, you simply knew that you wanted a cool lifestyle and to make a lot of money. That gets you nowhere except being a traffic fighter for life. At the end of this exercise, you now (hopefully) know:

- The exact lifestyle you want, including the exact house you want to live in and the car you want to drive.
- Precisely how much money you need to do what you want.
- A clear, ultimate business goal defined by actual math to reach your monetary goal.
- Five clear-cut goals you must achieve to reach this ultimate monetary goal.
- Smaller goals that make reaching your five larger goals simple and straightforward with clear action steps.

Literally the only thing left to do is to take the small actions you have laid out in this exercise and solve the problems they will naturally create. You have essentially built a train track to your goals. Instead of simply wanting them, you now know how to get them. You have defined your dreams and your goals and written the map to achieve them.

Imagine before this exercise that you were a painter trying to paint an exact picture of a building that does not yet exist in real life, but you had only a hazy description of what it should look like. Your job would be nearly impossible, because there aren't any clear actions—or in this case, brush strokes—to reach this goal. Now imagine trying to paint the same building with a paint-by-number blueprint provided for you. It would be quite easy as long as you stick with the directions. This is what we are doing here.

At the end of this book, we will go into much more detail about this exact topic. What you need to know for now is that the better you get at performing this exercise, the clearer getting rich will become. All wealthy people are experts at imagining a far-off goal and defining every step to get there. If you want to become rich, you must start thinking less in vague wants and more in defined goals.

OVERWHELMED? APPLY THE SIXTH PILLAR (FORGETTING "WHAT IF" AND FOCUSING ON "WHAT IS")

There's a very good chance that you had a lot of trouble with the exercise in this chapter. You can probably identify how much money you need, but you might have no idea how you want to make that money, or you might not be able to come up with all the action steps needed to create your business and make all of that money.

At the end of this book, I have set aside an entire chapter to discuss business ideas, which will give you very clear-cut directions on how to start creating an income. With that being said, if you paid attention to the sixth pillar, then you should know that the only thing you should be focusing on is your most immediate problem, which is choosing how to make money.

If you read this chapter but could not decide on a route to choose, that is perfectly okay. The point of this chapter is to get you to understand the goal-setting exercise and how wealthy people set goals. What I highly suggest you do is to keep reading the rest of the pillars and then start tackling the problem of how to make money once you get to the business ideas section of this book. You still need to learn the final pillars before you can appropriately choose the hows and whys of becoming rich.

With that in mind, the eighth pillar is all about how to maximize the income from our actions. It should clear up a lot of the what-ifs you had about this chapter.

(Note: I did not do a beginner and veteran section in this chapter because defining your goals and mapping them out is the same no matter who you are or what your experience level is.)

THE 8TH PILLAR

FOCUSING SOLELY ON WHAT GETS YOU PAID

I want you to imagine something completely ridiculous with me. Let's envision that you are in some ass-backwards reality where you get paid $1,000 every time you walk, jog, or run one mile. Like clockwork, every time your body moves 5,280 feet, there is a "cha-ching" noise, and a thousand buckaroos go straight into your bank account. Let's also imagine that you can only do this for eight hours a day total. And on top of that, anything that counts as preparing for walking, jogging, or running also counts as work and cannot be done outside of those eight hours a day.

Now I want you to answer me this: What is the single most important action that you should be doing to make money?

The answer might seem obvious and simple at first. Say it with me: Running as fast as possible. However, if we think about it for a few minutes, there are hundreds of other things that we must do. Things such as:

- Cooking carb-loaded food so we can run for a long time without needing a break.
- Shopping for food.
- Eating all of this food.
- Preparing water stops on our running routes.
- Buying running clothes and shoes and replacing running clothes and shoes.
- Washing running clothes (unless you're the confidently smelly type).

- Finding new running methods to run faster without getting more tired.
- Obtaining, measuring, and taking daily supplements.

These are just off the top of my head; there are definitely dozens more. However, while these are required for us to reach our goal of making money by running as fast as possible, they actually subtract from the amount of money we are making.

Let's imagine that we have to spend thirty minutes preparing food and setting up water on our route every day. If we were able to spend that time running, that would generate $6,000 (at a five-minute mile) per day. This means we lose about $180,000 (including weekends) every single month just from preparing food and setting up water. That's over $1 million a year. That's absurd!

There is a simple solution to this, though: hire someone to prepare our food and set up our water routes for $20 a day. This way, the only time we have to waste is eating the food and drinking the water. (This could further be eliminated by simply strapping an IV to ourselves to pump nutrients into our body throughout the day, but let's stick with the human-helper example for now.) If we hired a food and water preparer, we would be able to make $179,400 MORE each month simply by paying someone a little over $600 a month.

I think you are starting to get the point. In order to make as much money as possible, every moment of our time should be spent focusing on what gets us paid, which, in this case, is running. But we can focus on anything that increases our running speed that can't be delegated, as long as it gets us a high ROI. For example, we couldn't delegate a shoe fitting, right? So if the opportunity comes up for us to try a brand-new elite pair of running shoes that guarantee to help us run faster, it would be well worth the time spent doing it, since better shoes that help us run faster mean we can make more money.

Long story short, running is what gets us paid, so running is solely what we focus on. We do not do anything except run unless it helps us with running faster/more/better and can't be outsourced like the example above. Everything that *can* be delegated—such as cooking our food and cleaning our clothes—*must* be delegated. This is the single easiest way to make as much money as quickly as possible.

YOU ARE ONLY ONE PERSON, AND ONE PERSON CAN ONLY DO SO MUCH . . . UNLESS THEY ARE IN CONTROL OF A GIANT BUSINESS ROBOT

At this moment in time, you can only put in 60 to 80 hours a week (or maybe 120 hours if you never eat or shower) into working on your dreams. This might seem like a lot, but to any serious entrepreneur, this number is laughable. Every single day, at least 100 hours of work are put into my dreams. How is this possible? Because I am not the only person working.

As I just mentioned, putting in 80 hours of work each week is simply not a lot of time, but if you have ten employees, you could easily put in 400 hours of work per week (ten people working 40 hours per week equals 400 hours per week). In fact, a person who works 10 hours a week but intelligently directs the 400 work hours of his employees will get so much more work accomplished than he could alone.

One of the main focuses of the eighth pillar of wealth is recognizing this anomaly. No matter who you are, you are just one person who can only learn so many skills and can only put in so many hours of work each day. With the right people, though, you become something far greater. Think of it almost like sitting inside the head of a giant Transformer robot. By yourself, you cannot do much. But once you are controlling the machine, you can push over a skyscraper.

So many entrepreneurs fail to understand this idea, and it restricts their growth for years. They feel like they are the only ones who can handle certain tasks, and they view bringing other people on as expensive and unnecessary. But, if you hire the right people, every employee could make you ten times what you pay them. On top of that, every person you bring to your team results in your decisions having farther and farther reach. In fact, it will come to the point where the best investment of your time is directing other people, because every decision leads to hundreds of hours of progress.

If I give a software developer $30,000, I can almost guarantee that the software will generate $300,000. On top of this, I simply do not have the time to learn how to develop software like they already know how to do. My time needs to be spent selling and directing people. This gives me great power, though, because instead of having to spend hundreds of hours learning code, I can simply tell my team "make it so," and it results in hundreds of hours of progress in a week or two. This is lightning in a bottle as long as I make the right decisions.

FOR THOSE OF US WHO DO NOT MAGICALLY GENERATE MONEY BY RUNNING

While no one can magically pump money into their bank account by running up and down the street all day, we can drastically increase the money we make by applying the mind-set shown in the example above. What you need to take away from this story is that by identifying the actions that get the highest ROI and solely focusing on them, we can get paid faster and increase our income.

In the above situation, it is pretty easy to identify what we should focus on: running. However, when it comes to making money, especially when we are starting out, knowing what we should be doing is much more confusing. However, if we can narrow down the few actions that make us money and simply focus on them, we can drastically cut the amount of time it takes to become profitable.

When many people get started, they are all over the place with their actions. They are reading self-help books, doing research on ten different things at once, and essentially flopping around like a horny fish. Their actions are very ineffective because they are not doing what will actually make them money.

To repeat myself for the nine-hundredth time, you need to find out the one (or two or three) thing(s) that will make you money in your business. Most of the time, this thing will be selling, but as I've mentioned before, even that can be broken down into other, smaller actions. Focusing on other things lowers the amount of time that you are able to concentrate on your main moneymakers. Just like preparing our own food in the running analogy, these are not only wastes of time but, in effect, income stealers.

Let me explain this from a business point of view.

In my business, there are three things that generate the most income. If I spend all day, every day doing these things, I get richer and richer. These are generating leads, selling in webinars, and creating sales material to send to people.

The easiest way for my business to increase our ROI is to increase the amount of leads coming in for under $5 each. If I get five hundred leads a day, I make $15,000 extra a day on average. If I crack it up to a thousand, I make $30,000 a day on average. I have automated everything else in my business, so the number-one way to get a return on my time is by increasing the amount of leads coming in.

On top of this, for every hour that I am directly selling on a webinar, I average about $30,000 to $50,000 per hour of work. This is outrageously high, and because of this, I need to spend every second possible getting people to sign up for webinars and then selling to them.

Finally, for every hour I put into creating sales material, I make about $4,000 in return or more. Because of this, when I am not generating leads or selling on a webinar, I am crafting sales material for my business. The rest of my time is spent delegating out work to my many employees. For every fifteen minutes of delegating to employees, I get hundreds of hours out of them. Again, this is an extremely high ROI for my time.

Do you see how I am able to focus my time (and delegate everything I possibly can) to get the highest return? This is what the eighth pillar is all about, and this is how the richest people on earth get richer and richer. It is also how broke people and traffic fighters can get rich in the shortest time possible. To be as wealthy as you want to be, you must focus on what gets you paid and delegate the rest.

WATCH OUT! THE SAME ACTIONS THAT MAKE YOU WEALTHY CAN STOP YOU FROM BECOMING WEALTHIER

Once you become successful, you might realize that the actions that used to make you rich will actually stop you from becoming richer. They might keep you at the same level of wealth, but always remember this fact: you can't do the same things over and over again and expect different results. So, if you do something that generates $100,000 a month, you can't keep doing the same exact tasks and then expect to eventually generate $200,000 per month. Because of this, I have created a neat-o (yes, I just said "neat-o") system that you can use no matter what your income level is to identify your highest ROI actions while removing your lowest ROI actions. (There will also be no beginner or veteran sections in this chapter, because this system is applied the same way regardless of your experience.)

Let's start from the perspective of a complete beginner opening a marketing services business. Her name is Amy, and her first goal is to make $10,000 per month.

Now, what Amy must first do is write down the big goals that were set in the previous chapters. Her goal is to make $10,000 per month, and in order to do that, she figures out that she must get ten clients at $1,000 per month each.

Big Goal:

Reach $10,000 a month in income by getting ten clients at $1,000 per month.

Next, Amy needs to write out her goals and tasks that she wants to get done this month. Since she is a beginner, Amy has a ton of goals that veteran marketers have already accomplished.

Goals for the Month:

- Read four marketing books
- Work on ranking SEO websites for practice
- Learn AdWords and Facebook advertising
- Create a business website
- Cold call and e-mail potential clients

The cool thing about being a beginner is that almost every action you take is going to have an ROI of some sort. This is why it is so critical to take as much action as possible when you start. With that being said, only one of Amy's goals generates any money.

What Amy needs to do now is to go through each of her goals and ask herself, "How much of an impact will this goal have on my big goal?"

Read four marketing books: While reading books might help her become better at selling, this will take a total of at least twenty-eight hours of time (seven hours per book). This does not directly generate any income, and this task will not directly get her to $10,000 per month. This does not mean that she should never study selling material; she just needs to focus more on applying the sales training she learns instead of simply learning as much as she possibly can just for the sake of learning.

Work on ranking SEO websites for practice: While this will help Amy provide her service better, it will not get her paid, which means it will not get her any closer to making $10,000 per month.

Learn AdWords and Facebook advertising: Again, learning does not get us paid. No one is going to give Amy a check to learn how to advertise.

Create a business website: Websites without customers do not generate any money. This, again, is a waste of time and something that could easily be outsourced or delegated to someone on your team.

Cold call and e-mail potential clients: This is the only action that directly leads to getting paid. If Amy spends eight hours a day trying to get clients on the phone or to respond in e-mail, she will have the highest possible chance of actually getting clients. If she gets one client every 15 hours of work, she should be able to land ten clients through her 160 hours of work (a full work month).

At this rate, this task is the *only* task she has time to focus on if she wants ten clients by the end of the month.

THE END. GOOD GAME. TIME TO GET TO WORK.

Look at the example above. While all the other tasks seem like relevant objectives, none of them actually correlate directly to Amy making any money. The only thing that gets her paid and gets her close to her big goal is a client giving her a check. That's it. Nothing else gets her paid. Her highest ROI action is selling to clients, and she should be doing this every waking hour of every day.

A QUICK NOTE FOR BEGINNERS

This might sound insane, but it is exactly what you must do if you are a beginner who needs money. If you want to start making money fast, you have to focus only on the actions that get you paid. It is not necessarily a mistake, but I see beginners who need money *now* spend countless hours on learning, reading books about the topic at hand, and essentially doing everything all at once. Understand this: Doing something like reading a book now might get you paid more a month from now. Picking up the phone and getting a client (or doing only actions that generate income) now will get you paid *today*. Also understand that you will be learning far more from "doing" (actions) than you will ever learn from "learning about doing." Trust me, if you know a topic well enough, get out there and get paid.

(Side note: After reading the statement above, you might wonder, what is the point of reading this book? By this logic, it would be best to just get out there and start doing! This is 100 percent right; however, "doing" aimlessly and without the right core mind-sets can be a fruitless endeavor. The reason this book is so vital is because it gives you the beliefs and mind-sets that will allow your actions to be ten times more effective and help you to make the right choices without having to experience the hardships that most entrepreneurs go through.)

BACK TO THE TOPIC AT HAND

As I mentioned before, however, the actions that make us rich as a beginner will keep us from getting richer as a successful entrepreneur. Let me explain.

Let's imagine that Amy has now signed ten clients and is making $10,000 per month. Great! She also hired someone for 30 percent of the revenue to provide the service so she can focus solely on selling.

Her new goal is to make $100,000 per month, which means that she needs a hundred clients to pay her $1,000 monthly. The issue is that, with a rate of one client per fifteen hours of work, she can only sign ten new clients a month. It will take her quite a while to reach $100,000 per month, especially if some of her clients drop off like they naturally do in most businesses.

What Amy needs to do now is to write down all of her current selling actions, which got her to ten clients, and define what is truly getting her paid. This time, though, she needs to define how many hours she generally devotes to them.

Goals for the month:
- Make five hundred cold calls (forty hours).

- Send and respond to a thousand emails (forty hours).
- Make two hundred and fifty follow-up calls (forty hours).
- Close the deal in one-on-one meetings (forty hours).

Again, let's go through these goals and see how they correlate to Amy getting paid. Remember, this is exactly what she did to get to $10,000 per month. Sadly, these goals will not get her to $100,000 per month, and here's why.

Make five hundred cold calls: While cold calling can lead to one-on-one meetings, it will not directly get Amy paid. *Yes,* this action got her paid in the beginning, and she needed to do it when she first started, because not only did she not have any money to outsource this task, cold calling actually did help her get a few clients. But now that she needs a hundred clients to reach her new goal, cold calling will be too time consuming and will not provide the ROI needed to hit her goal.

Send and respond to a thousand emails: This has the same issue as making cold calls. It might get her meetings, but it is time consuming and will not directly get her paid.

Make two hundred and fifty follow-up calls: Same issue again. Making follow-up calls will not directly get her paid.

Close the deal in one-on-one meetings: This is where Amy gets the check and gets paid. In fact, in almost half of the meetings (which are about an hour long) she attends, she seals the deal. This means that for every two hours in a meeting, she gets one new client. That's $500 per hour worked.

With the facts above, what task should Amy be doing to get to $100,000 a month? It is pretty obvious that she needs to solely be in one-on-one closing meetings every minute of every day. This task generates $500 per hour, and at 160 hours of work a month, it will add $80,000 monthly to her revenue! Since this is recurring income that stacks on itself, this means she could well surpass $100,000 a month in as little as five or six weeks. At the very least, though, she has increased her value per time so much that she can generate $100,000 per month.

So, what else does Amy need to do? Easy. She needs to hire a team of people to do her cold calling, e-mailing, and follow-up calling. Her employees will be able to make enough calls and send enough e-mails for Amy that she will be able to be in meetings for exactly eight hours a day.

Bing, bang, boom, our friend is now making $100,000 per month.

See the pattern? Identify high ROI actions and remove low ROI actions from your daily routine. We can apply the exercise over and over again to obtain more and more money. When we are frustrated with our income and not sure how to increase it, we just need to write out our goals and identify which ones are not directly creating the ROI we need. We can then either stop doing them completely or hire someone to do them for us.

BILLIONAIRES' ROI OF THEIR ACTIONS IS ASTRONOMICAL

Over my time of researching and following some of the richest people on earth, I have noticed that they are all masters of choosing how to spend their time.

You won't see Mark Zuckerberg coding software; there's no way a single coder could generate a net worth of $26 billion. Instead, you will see Mark finding ways to get more users while leading a team of a thousand developers to multiply the ROI a thousand times on every action he takes.

You won't see Warren Buffet leading a single company. That would not generate enough money fast enough. You will see him investing and guiding two hundred companies at the same time so that he is reaping two hundred times the reward for his time.

While we can certainly increase the amount we charge per hour or per item we sell, the easiest way to increase your ROI is by hiring other people so we can focus on our main task. A man with a thousand employees (or freelancers) performing actions can create a seismic earthquake-like ripple of ROI, but one man alone can work only as much as he can physically work. This is where the ninth pillar comes in.

THE 9TH PILLAR

PEOPLE GIVE MONEY TO PEOPLE THAT GET PEOPLE

Prepare yourself, because I am about to lay some Bruce Willis, *The Sixth Sense* revelations on you. Ready? Okay, here it is . . .

Money is not real.

Well, at least not in the way many people view it. Think about it. If you were the only person on earth, money would have no value or use. And, at this current moment in human evolution, money does not tangibly exist in some circumstances. Just look at the stock market. Those numbers going up and down on a computer screen can make a man more powerful than a Greek god or more worthless than an unbathed hobo, yet they're just computer signals on a screen. Those numbers and pieces of paper are given such power because people give them power. Because of this, you literally cannot become rich without other people, because in order for someone to be rich, other people need to exist to give you the power of being rich. (They also need to exist to give you the money, obviously.)

What is money, then? Money is power over other people. More so, it is the exchange of power between people. A man signs a check, and he can get people to build his house. A woman signs a check, and she can get people to give her a car. A man signs a check, and people will catch a fish a thousand miles away, fly it to him, cook it, and serve it to him with some vegetables and a bottle of wine.

Money has power because it is perceived to have value, which is why you can trade it in exchange for groceries and clothes and motorcycles. The value of money comes from other people's belief that it has value (and power). Without this belief, money would not have value and would become meaningless. This is an essential understanding because once you believe this idea, you will stop focusing on money and focus more on understanding the people that give money its value (and how to get them to give you their money).

In order to obtain any money at all, you need other people. More so, you need these people to want to give you their money. So, the true secret to making money is getting people to do what you want (which is to give you their money). To do this, you need to gain control over them or persuade them (in a good way).

In short, if you are trying to get rich, you are actually trying to gain control over other people. If you start to think like this, then you will start to discover how to become wildly successful.

This is what this pillar is all about: people. But it's also about getting out of the mind-set of viewing money as just money. Thinking like this is a surefire way to miss out on the most valuable lessons of wealth creation.

Over the course of whatever the hell you decide to do, people are going to decide whether you are successful or not. The sole factor of how successful you are is how good you are at influencing and controlling other people's decisions. While you are influencing and controlling other people's decisions, you will constantly have other people attempting to control your decisions as well. How you react, judge, and influence people is going to be the most important factor of your success.

Because of this, you must realize that a person who is wealthy is a person who understands people. You see, one of the biggest mistakes of past traffic fighters is that they try to make money without understanding people. They think that money is generated by doing a task, and that money comes out of some magic money wormhole that is linked to their bank account. Every dollar anyone has ever made originally came from another person's bank account and was the result of a trade of perceived value.

Many people fail to understand this when they start a business, and they therefore try to forge a business without thinking about people. They forget that they must lead people. They forget that they must persuade people. They forget that they must influence people first and foremost. They forget that they must have something that makes people want to give them money.

Think about Steve Jobs for a moment. Before we get further into this chapter, I want to make sure that you don't confuse this pillar with being liked. According to most movies and documentaries, Steve Jobs, for the most part, was disliked, and lots of people considered him an asshole. Sure, people loved and idolized him as a businessman and for his products, but if you look into what he was like as a person, it was far from likable. There are tons of people we like, but this does not mean that we just start handing them $20 bills every time we see them. What Steve had was different; he understood what people wanted before they wanted it, and because of this, people wanted to give him money.

Steve understood people like the back of his hand. He knew what made them tick, what made them intrigued, and what made them spend loads of money. He knew how to get people to do what he wanted them to do, whether it was his employees or his customers.

Who coded his products? Other people. Who engineered his products? Other people. Who built his products? Other people. Who built buzz around his products and his brand? Other people. Who bought all the products that paid for all of it? Other people.

In my opinion, Apple (formally led by Jobs) products are usually far behind other companies in terms of technology. They break a lot, they are generally not as innovative as other products, and there are much more advanced options out there. Yet Apple could always get people to hand over hundreds or thousands of dollars in exchange for a "cool new gadget."

This is the power of understanding people and how to push them to do what you want. You must realize that reaching your goals without being able to control people is impossible. You cannot become rich by yourself, and at the end of it, other people will have more to do with your wealth than you do.

Got it? Good!

WARNING: PEOPLE ARE SCARY, AND DEALING WITH THEM IS DIFFICULT

Now, before we start, the goal of this chapter is not to train you to be a charismatic leader of man and a champion of sales. The goal is to alert you to and make you brutally aware of this pillar. All too often, people try to become rich while never leaving their "people comfort zone" (meaning they don't treat people any differently or learn how other people think). You *have* to understand how important people are to your success and how vital it is to really understand them.

Once again, this doesn't mean that you have to be personally likable, and it doesn't even mean that you must like other people. You can be mean, rude, and unappealing in your personal life, but you must understand people and know how to make them do what you want them to do in order to become successful. That's just the truth.

Okay, I think I repeated myself enough. The question now is: How does understanding people translate into making money? If you figure out what your target audience wants and needs, how does that make them hand over cash in exchange for whatever you're selling? Well, there is *one* skill that is the liaison between knowing people and making money, and that is learning how to sell.

IF YOU LEARN ONE THING, LEARN HOW TO SELL

What you must understand is that at the core of gaining money, there is an interaction between two people. Whether it is via an Internet ad, a boardroom table, or a face-to-face handshake deal at Starbucks, there is always a party convincing another party to spend some money. No business deal happens without this interaction.

With that in mind, the most important part of any business is selling. There are horrible, semiworthless products that have made millions of dollars, and there are amazing products that have made close to nothing. It all comes down to how good you are at persuading others to give you money and be happy about giving you money.

Because of this, the quickest hack to "making it" is becoming amazing at selling. Now, selling can come in many forms. For example, I sell to thousands of people every day via advertising. Every single day, there are hundreds of thousands of little Alex clones (ads) selling to people on Facebook and YouTube. Those little clones sell the living hell out of stuff, too. This is because I understand how people will think and react and what they will do when they see my pages, ads, and videos.

Selling comes in a thousand shapes and forms, but at the core of it is understanding people and knowing how to influence their actions. Once you know that, everything becomes quite easy.

Opening a real estate business is easy because you understand what people really want and you know how to make people buy houses better than anyone else.

Running an online business is simple because your people-pleasing ads convert so highly and your products are impossible to say no to.

Starting a protein powder business is smooth sailing because your product and advertising influence potential customers more than your competitors' products.

Hitting $100,000 in profits per month from your SEO marketing service is child's play because you know how to convince multiple large companies to pay you $20,000 per month for your SEO consulting.

Selling makes everything easy. I kid you not, I know people who walk into massive corporations and leave with a $100,000 check every day of the week. This is because they know how to pull corporate people's heartstrings and make them feel like they are being presented with the cure for cancer. This is something you could do right now if you knew how to sell.

With that being said, *not* knowing how to sell can make every project you work on a living hell. This is why you don't want to leave selling up to someone else. Someone else can code your software. Someone else can make your products. Someone else can do just about anything for you. But no one else knows your product like you do, knows your target audience like you do, or cares about your ROI as much as you do. Therefore, no one can sell like you can.

The first line of every business is selling. A business's growth is determined by its sales. A business with a great product but no sales is a dead business. More than likely, if you are reading this book, you cannot sell (yet). If you could, you could start a real estate business tomorrow and close a $1 million deal this week. But since you (probably) can't do this (yet), becoming a master seller needs to be your number one priority.

(If you are interested in learning more about selling, stop by AlexBecker.org for a free course on selling and starting an online business.)

WEALTHY ENTREPRENEURS KNOW THAT EMOTIONS DRIVE PEOPLE

Mediocre entrepreneurs provide and sell products. Wildly successful entrepreneurs provide and sell emotions.

Other Search Engines vs. Google
Other Smart Phones vs. iPhone
Other Cars vs. Ferrari
Generic Coffee Shops vs. Starbucks
Generic Clothing Stores vs. Louis Vuitton
Every Other Energy Drink vs. Red Bull

In all of these situations, one brand is clearly the winner. The iPhone greatly outsells the BlackBerry. Everyone knows this, but if you ask them why, they wouldn't be able to give you a real answer. They might say something like, "iPhones are just cooler," or, "They're cutting edge," or, "They're easier to use." They will not tell you the technical specs or be able to explain why they're cutting edge or how they're easier to use. The truth is, the actual reason why people buy iPhones has nothing to do with the phone at all. It has to do with how the idea of owning it makes them feel, which is cool, connected, modern, and trendy.

This applies to so much more than selling, though. When you get ahold of people's emotions, people will unconsciously flock to you, and everyone will want a piece of what you have. The best employees will want to work for you, the most important people on earth will want to network with you, and consumers will line up for days to spend five times what your competition charges on a product that isn't even half as good. At the end of the day, people are ruled by their emotions and just want to feel positive, happy, and accepted by others.

So, what you need to do with this lesson is keep it in mind when you are choosing your industry, designing what you will sell, and especially when you start advertising and marketing. The easiest way to get an edge over everyone is not by having the best product but by having the product, brand, and messaging that makes people "feel" the most.

SPENDING TIME LEARNING ABOUT PEOPLE IS VITAL TO YOUR BUSINESS

Now that you are aware of this pillar, my best advice for you is to spend some time each day learning about people. Whether it is learning about selling, leading, or controlling emotions, you need to know it all, so just dive right in.

One thing I must mention is that understanding people can be used for good or evil. I am *not* telling you to understand people so that you can manipulate them into doing bad things or spend money on crappy products (like old cigarette commercials or literally any scam artist online). I am telling you to understand people so you can improve their lives while you, in turn, make a ton of money.

There's one other thing I must add. In the previous chapter, I discussed that you should only focus on things that directly get you paid and things that you couldn't delegate. Well, since selling is your main focus, learning how to sell better is also part of your main focus. So spending a little time each day learning how to understand people will result in more sales for you, a.k.a. more money.

With that being said, let's look at how to apply this pillar as a beginner versus a veteran of wealth creation.

HOW TO UNDERSTAND PEOPLE AS A BEGINNER

If you are a beginner at wealth creation, odds are that you just plain stink at understanding people. You don't know why people buy one product versus another. You probably don't like leaving your comfort zone and forcing yourself to meet new people. You more than likely hate the thought of selling and don't know the first step to getting someone to buy something.

I see it all the time. In fact, this is why so many people are attracted to Internet marketing. I no longer directly teach because I cannot stand to be around this mind-set. However, when I did, I noticed that people got into the whole "make money online in your underwear" craze not because they were lazy but because they wanted to make money without having to deal with anyone face to face.

In short, most beginners will try anything and everything to avoid having to understand people. Most people just want to be some shadow man who presses buttons and makes a ton of money. But this is not how it works. In fact, the reason why business owners and Internet marketers become so successful is because they understand people better than anyone else in their company.

Anyone can sit back and code or send an e-mail to a list of customers. It takes a leader to make all that work actually translate into people handing over tons of money.

Contrary to what you might be thinking at this very moment, it can be very easy to master this pillar (and benefit from it) if you are starting from scratch. It might actually be easier for you than for a business veteran because you don't have as many "business tactics" ingrained into your brain yet. You are starting fresh, which is great.

As a beginner, there are two things you need to focus on right now: selling and being comfortable with people (and leading them to do things). If you can do these two things, you are going to have a hard time not succeeding.

1. SELLING IS EVERYTHING

Business doesn't happen until somebody buys something. Simple, right? You can have the best product in the world or the worst, but it doesn't matter until someone actually buys it.

This means that you need to understand the ins and outs of selling as quickly as possible. As I mentioned earlier in the book, people learn best by diving headfirst into business. *But*, in this case, you must also supplement your experience with some outside learning from books and Internet courses. Just make sure that whatever you are learning or reading will directly help you to increase your sales and, in turn, increase the amount of money you make.

With that being said, I have included a list of the fifty best sales books ever written on my website, AlexBecker.org. Go check it out for my personal suggestions on what you should be reading.

2. BEING COMFORTABLE WITH PEOPLE

The next thing you need to do is learn how to be comfortable with people. This is actually quite simple. To become more comfortable with people, the only thing you need to do is force yourself into situations where you have to deal with people.

That's it. But, of course, that's easier said than done. Most people will shy away from cold calling or talking to strangers at a marketing event because they don't want to make a fool of themselves. What you need to understand is A) you probably *will* make a fool of yourself and B) that is totally okay.

The first time I ever attended an event, spoke at an event, talked to a client, approached a girl, approached a potential business partner, approached a mentor, etc., I was nervous as hell and did quite poorly. After doing this for years, though, I am pretty great at all of the above. Why? Because I simply did them over and over again, and eventually I got comfortable doing them. You might think you're socially awkward or you might even get anxiety in certain social situations, but if success is your goal, then you must push yourself and learn how to be comfortable (and charming) in these situations.

So, the biggest lesson I can pass onto you is this: be proactive about throwing yourself into challenging social situations. On top of that, *never* shy away from something that makes you feel socially uncomfortable. (Within reason, of course. There is no need to go attend a nudist event just to prove you can.) Doing uncomfortable things means that you are learning and growing, and this is necessary on your way to wealth and success.

That's it; it's that simple.

HOW TO UNDERSTAND PEOPLE AS A VETERAN

This might hurt to hear, but just because you have made some money in business does not mean that you understand people. (If you were truly great at understanding people, you would be so successful that you wouldn't need to read this book.) Most businesses are created around what the owner thinks is best, not what he or she thinks other people want.

I often see people create a great product or service, and then that's it. They might sell a few, they might even make decent money from it, but in reality, the product doesn't get people excited, and every part of the user experience is confusing or difficult.

To focus more on people, ask yourself these questions about your brand/product vision and your marketing.

Vision Questions: Are you the coolest solution out there? Are people passionate about your business? What does your business stand for? Is this the best version of your business you can envision? Would you honestly want to be your customer?

Marketing Questions: Who is your target customer? What's the best way to reach them? Do they actually respect you? Is your company fun to do business with? Do you explain the value of your product in your advertising? Do you focus on how your product will make your customers feel in your advertising?

I want you to take a step back and look at your business as a whole. Then think about what you would do if your goal were to simply break even and attract as many people as possible. We of course want to make a ton of money, but focusing on other people and their desires/emotions/needs is the key to expanding your business from something small to something huge. How can people connect with your product or brand? What emotion are you really trying to sell?

Look at Apple, Red Bull, Starbucks, Whole Foods, Comic-Con, etc. All of these businesses/events stand for something. They mean something to people beyond the product. They are a way of life or a feeling. These are prime examples of businesses that truly understand and connect with their customer base.

This is extremely hard to explain, but the biggest lesson I can teach you is that you must start thinking about people and their feelings as the biggest picture. You must think of how you present yourself to them and the emotions that are generated when they think about your brand. And, as a veteran to creating wealth, this means that you probably have to change quite a few things about your brand and marketing.

Let me give you an example of how I applied the above to one of my businesses.

With my SEO business, the cost of getting a lead was getting way too high in my industry. My employees and I tried everything to lure people in and get them to give us their e-mail addresses. It kept getting more and more expensive, because at the end of the day, people don't want to be lured in. We were only thinking about people as numbers and focusing on the business (and our income) first.

What people want in the SEO industry is to make more money and to be able to buy trustworthy services. So, instead of trying to bribe them with a classic e-mail opt-in bait, I simply gave them what they wanted.

I created a 100 percent free marketplace that allowed SEO buyers and sellers to come together. This marketplace gave them every tool they needed to sell more and every tool they needed to find the best SEO services. Then, I even flooded the market with traffic to get it started.

Competitors of mine had tried something similar in the past, except it was not free to use, and the business took huge chunks of money from the sellers. Because of this, the sellers did not want to open up shop there. Plain and simple.

Instead, I not only decided to make mine 100 percent free but I also gave sellers and people that promoted the marketplace a 20 percent commission on anything they sold. I gave people exactly what they wanted, which was the ability to make more money and buy the right services. I understood them, and because of this, I was able to know (and give them) exactly what they wanted.

The result? Tens of thousands of users in the marketplace, all coming in as fresh leads to our business. Even crazier, sellers began running advertising to our marketplace, effectively giving us the leads we used to pay a huge amount for completely for free. These were leads we could then bring into our business and turn into customers. Essentially, we were getting new customers to our business with no hard cost to obtain them.

This almost doubled the amount of sales I was able to create in our business, *and* it dropped our advertising cost to zero. See how that worked? Instead of thinking about my business and what I wanted, I tried to understand people and what they wanted.

Now, what I suggest is that you remember this short lesson and start applying it to your business every day. On top of that, start researching why the most popular brands create such loyal followings. You will find that it rarely has to do with the product.

Last, if you are a veteran and want to take your business to the next level, I have included a list of the twenty-five best books on improving your business via understanding people at my website, AlexBecker.org/booklist.

NO ONE EVER GOT RICH UNTIL SOMEONE ELSE PAID THEM ENOUGH MONEY TO MAKE THEM RICH

Get it? Good! This is a pretty simple pillar, and I can only beat a dead horse so many times. In this chapter, we have discussed how we can "control" other people. In the next pillar, we will talk about how other people can affect us and how we can use their influence to drive ourselves to do incredible things.

THE 10TH PILLAR
FINDING COMPETITIVE FRIENDS AND SUITABLE MENTORS

This pillar is a two-part pillar. Almost all of the other pillars in this book have to do with mind-set shifts, but this pillar is a physical life hack that you can use to make money without even changing your thought process. While I do *not* recommend doing that, I just need you to understand how powerful this pillar is.

Let's jump straight into part one.

FIND COMPETITIVE FRIENDS

In part one, I want to talk about one of the dumbest yet greatest experiences of my life: playing World of Warcraft (WoW) . . . for hundreds and hundreds of hours. I assume that if I had devoted these hundreds and hundreds of hours to work instead of video games, I would be worth about ten times what I am worth right now. But that's besides the point. The reason I want to talk about WoW is because it is a true testament to the first part of the tenth pillar.

If you don't know what WoW is, then let me fill you in, because the effect this "game" has on people's lives is comedically dramatic. You see, WoW is a massively multiplayer online role-playing game (MMORPG). An MMO involves playing a game with thousands of other people at the same time, and an RPG means, well, that you're pretending to be someone else on the screen the whole time.

While you are having a lovely dinner at home every night, there are thousands of people interacting in online-hosted cities and living in a land made up of Internet servers. I look back and smile at being a part of this experience, because I was truly part of an online world and community . . . one very different than the one I'm currently involved with.

Now, the goal of WoW is to get better weapons and items to help your character fight better. On top of that, the more you fight, the stronger your character gets by "leveling up." For example, a person who is at level 5 wouldn't even come close to beating someone at level 70 (the highest level) in a fight. Then, once you hit the highest level, WoW becomes all about who collects the best gear. Gear has levels just like the characters, but to save time, let's just sum it up by saying if you have better gear than the other people at your level, you can destroy them in a fight.

Now, here is the thing about WoW. Getting to the highest level and having a moderately strong character takes months of full-time playing (yes, I mean between eight and ten hours per day). You could sit at your computer for forty hours straight and barely make any progress. I can tell you from experience that this is not fun, but it is extremely addictive. In fact, it is so addictive that, at one point, WoW had over fourteen million players paying nineteen dollars a month to play the game. On top of that, about five million of these players reached high levels because they played A LOT. At any time, you could jump on a server and there would be thousands of people running through the cities who were at the max level.

Now, let's take a step back and remember that most people are not experts at any one thing, and most people quit new endeavors once they get a little bit challenging. Seriously, our society is filled with bunches of people who have never followed through on anything. Guitar, books, fitness, success—you name it, and people will find a way to make a half-assed effort at it even though they really want to succeed (or they say they do, at least).

The insane thing about WoW is that it's able to take people from all walks of life and get them to work *hard* at something for hundreds or even thousands of hours. If you put this amount of work into anything, you will become an expert at it. The thing is that most people "can't" do that because of time restriction, laziness, or other priorities. However, the second you get them hooked to WoW, they can stay up for twenty hours straight working on their character and fighting strangers. See the messed up logic here?

Imagine if, right after reading this book, you spent every waking minute working at getting rich like a psycho. Seriously, picture waking up, turning on your computer, working for twenty hours, and stopping only to pee and eat whatever food you own that doesn't need to be cooked, then passing out from exhaustion and waking up four hours later to do it all over again. Then imagine doing this for months and months without taking breaks or vacations or even weekends off.

If you put that much time and effort into making money, you would have no problem getting rich. In fact, you'd have no problem getting anything you want in life. Unfortunately, this level of obsession is very hard to trigger . . . unless you know how to trigger it. WoW definitely knows how to trigger it. Do you want to know how to trigger it? Do you? DO YOU?! Okay, okay. I'll tell you.

Being in a community of like-minded people with the same goal will trigger an obsession to work hard, succeed, and compete (in a friendly way, usually).

Humans are like pack animals, and every single person wants recognition from their pack. When we find the group that we want to be in, we also start acting like them so we can "blend in" and feel like we are a part of that group. Therefore, you are going to act like the people whom you spend the most time with.

When you first start playing WoW, you are thrust into the game and thrown into a society where you are at the bottom of the social ladder. When you are in the game, you see super-decked-out, high-level characters in the city, and they naturally garner respect. In order to be one of the cool kids and do the cool stuff in the game, you have to get to that respected level, which means you must play the game for hours and hours . . . and even more hours. Not only that; the more you play, the more people you meet, need to work with, and need to fight. This causes you to become extremely competitive, and it will make you constantly desire to play more and get better.

In short, by playing WoW and being surrounded by people that play WoW, you will quickly become competitive and feel the need to keep up.

This effect cannot only change a person, it can become absolutely addictive and cause the WoW twenty-hour-a-day work effect that I spoke about earlier. As you can guess, this doesn't happen only in WoW; you will see similar things happen in sports, business, etc.

Wealthy people understand this and forcefully take advantage of it. Now, think of all the people you talk to on a regular basis. How many of them own their own businesses? How many are successful? How many are millionaires? How many are multimillionaires?

If your answer is, "Not many," then this is one of the big reasons that you are not wealthy. You know the expression, "You are what you eat"? Well, this is pretty similar (except please don't eat your friends). In this case, the saying is, "You are who you hang out with." The thing is, though, that most people are losers at generating wealth, and they hang out with other losers at generating wealth. I am here to tell you that solely hanging out with unsuccessful people, or people who aren't at the level you want to reach, will not be helpful for you on your road to success.

If you spend most of your time with people who don't care about making money and spend all of their free time sitting around the house watching reality TV, then you are more than likely going to do the same, because you want to fit in and because you have very little motivation to do things that no one around you is doing. You will have very little urge to make money or improve yourself because you are already on the same "level" as your pack.

On the flip side, if you spend most of your time with people who are making a million dollars a year or are working towards becoming rich, you are going to develop a strong urge to do the same. You are going to want to be part of their conversations and be their equal. They are competitive in their niches, so you'll want to be competitive in your niche. This would be like walking into a room in WoW and finding that everyone is at level 70. In order to be relevant or even noticed, you have to level up.

In addition, once you are surrounded by a certain type of person, not only will you become motivated and start to enjoy what they do, you will also naturally grow with them. In WoW, you will constantly see a group of people start at level 1 together and reach *much* higher levels by working together. The same applies with money and really any aspect of life (working out, playing basketball, learning calculus, etc.).

Almost every moment of my day is spent in contact with people who are hell-bent on making money. While I do have unsuccessful friends, the majority of the people I communicate with the most are entrepreneurs. In fact, outside of my family and my high school friends, I only communicate with people who are entrepreneurs.

This is how the world works, and you must take advantage of this idea if you want to become rich. If you want to learn how to speak French, the fastest way is to practice speaking French with other people who know how to speak French or who are also learning French. If you want to make money, you must talk to people who already have money or are also in the process of creating wealth.

The question now is, "How do you do this?" And, good for us, it's actually fairly simple.

PEOPLE ARE DYING TO MEET SIMILAR PEOPLE

When I first explain this pillar to people, they usually think I am telling them to *only* make a bunch of megamillionaire buddies. I am not. While having friends who are more successful than you will help you to become more motivated and successful and to fit in with them, it is also just as important to make friends with people who are in your exact position right now. This will allow you to form a bond that helps you all grow and learn together.

If you want to become part of the 1 percent of society who makes good (well, amazing) money, you *must* start interacting with people in that 1 percent, or at least with those people who are trying to join that 1 percent. Luckily, most niches have forums, Facebook groups, clubs, meetup groups, and huge live events that you can join or attend to meet like-minded people.

For example, if you want to get started by selling marketing services to companies, there are about a hundred Facebook groups and forums you can join with a few simple searches. Embed yourself in these groups and make sure you participate by writing comments, asking questions, and building relationships.

YOU MIGHT HAVE TO PAY FOR COMMUNITY (BUT THAT COULD BE A GOOD THING)

What you are going to find out very quickly is that there are all sorts of people selling courses and membership sites to help you learn how to make money in all sorts of ways. What you need to understand is how to know which of these groups and opportunities are useless and stupid and which are helpful and organized.

When it comes to paying to join an online group of like-minded people, the price sometimes dictates the actual value. This is similar to anything in life. Unsuccessful people who are content being unsuccessful are going to hang out at lower-priced venues, and higher-level people are usually going to hang out in higher-priced venues. The quality of people you are going to find at these different places is going to be radically different.

For example, I pay around $50,000 a year to be in a group led by one of my mentors. This group has made me millions of dollars and it has built some of the most beneficial connections I currently have in my life. I have surrounded myself with extremely competitive and successful friends who are able to push me to higher levels and elevate my thinking.

But I am not telling you to go join a $50,000 a year group right now. What I encourage you to do is join as many free groups as possible . . . right now. Then, pinpoint the "leaders" in the group and find out where they hang out (because trust me, the people leading those free groups are definitely in paid, higher-quality groups so they can become more successful). Make friends with them and ask them what they personally suggest.

The thing about free groups is that while some people are there to learn, many are simply there to try to sell their products. Be wary of these people, and rarely listen to their advice. In most cases, these groups are the blind leading the blind or the semiblind trying to sell half-assed information to the blind. But I do suggest you start with the free groups to attempt to meet other like-minded newbies and to also find out where the leaders hang out. Then, once you find a paid group in your niche of people on your level and higher, build relationships with as many people as possible and really use these groups to learn tips and to develop motivation.

The big point I am trying to make is that paying for groups or membership sites can be insanely helpful if you join the right one(s) with like-minded people. They don't necessarily have to be on the exact same level as you moneywise; their attitudes, ambition, and goals matter most. Just be sure to go off what real people are saying and pay less attention to the sales pitches coming your way.

MAKE FRIENDS AND COMPARE NOTES

Once you join a group (or five) and start talking to some people, my next advice is that you develop a group of friends with whom you regularly communicate and share information. Right now, the world you live in is probably not open to the idea of becoming rich. If you cannot go up to your group of friends and talk about making money without being met with skepticism or disinterest, you are in a damaging group. Quickly pull yourself out of that group and start networking with people who are excited to "talk money" and "talk business" with you.

If these people are in the same niche as you, there will be two huge advantages for you. First, you will have someone with whom to compete (which will cause you both to succeed quicker) and share your successes. I cannot stress how beneficial it is to have someone who can help push you forward. Second, you will have someone with whom to share notes and learn. The progress they make will be freely shared with you and vice versa. This will allow you guys to leapfrog each other for even faster results.

BE A GOOD FRIEND AND A JEALOUS ASSHOLE AT THE SAME TIME

Some people, such as Martin Luther King, Jr., Gandhi, etc., are naturally born with a relentless desire to be great and change the world. These are all selflessly driven people. If you look at other greats, though, often one of their greatest motivators is kicking the shit out of other people and rubbing their faces in it or simply proving people wrong. If you ever hear these people talk, there is quite a bit of anger and focus on beating others and being the best.

If you're reading this book, you probably don't fall into the first category, and that is completely okay. Like I stated before in this book, humans are not motivated by surface-level crap, and this is especially true when you are just starting out. The honest truth is that deep emotions such as anger, jealousy, and a desire to beat the crap out of other people are some of the strongest motivators you can bring into your life *if* you focus them the right way.

You have to understand that emotions are neither innately good nor innately bad. When Michael Jordan got his butt whooped in a game, he got angry, and then he focused ten times harder on his next game. This is good. When a traffic fighter gets pissed off, he cusses out people on YouTube and takes it out on his friends. This is bad. Notice the huge difference in how a winner uses emotions versus a traffic fighter.

One of the best parts about having competitive friends and surrounding yourself with winners is that they will help you to create these emotions. The biggest mistake I see, though, is people failing to use these emotions for good. Imagine if Jordan never cared about losing a game and never let that loss force him to try harder the next game. I doubt he would be the sports legend he is today. In fact, he probably would have never become a professional athlete in the first place. The same applies to you.

Perhaps one of my most respected entrepreneur friends has a business in the exact same niche as I do. He is also one of my most brutal competitors in this niche and, in my opinion, he is a wee bit smarter than me. I consider him a friend and will personally help him out with anything. But, on the business battlefield, we are at war. And yes, I get extremely pissed off when he beats me, and I get jealous if he makes advances before I do.

This is actually a good thing, because this competition has forced both of us to up our games to such a high level that no one else can compete with us. We have pushed each other from having ragtag companies to being very refined tech entrepreneurs. It is unlikely that I would have the skills I have today if it weren't for him constantly breathing down my neck in the business world.

Thankfully, we are both launching new tech companies that can work together, and I believe that both companies could make $100 million per year each.

See how focusing my emotions the right way and allowing myself to be almost childishly competitive with my friends has pushed me to go way farther than I could on my own? I know that this sounds a little immature, but if you can find ways to use your friends and competitors to bring this emotional, jealous, passionate drive out of you, you are going to have a severe advantage over your noncompetitive "competitors."

Pretty simple, right?

Everything I just went over is something you probably already knew in the back of your mind. But, there is a second part to this pillar, and it is another huge cheat code when it comes to cracking success.

PART TWO: FIND APPROPRIATE MENTORS

Finding competitive and successful friends is important, but there is another important person (or group of people) with whom you need to form a relationship: appropriate mentors. For whatever reason, many people try to reach massive success on their own without personal mentors. Maybe they think they're smart enough to do it on their own. Maybe they are afraid to ask for help. Maybe they have no idea how to find a mentor. Most of the time, they just do not know how important having a mentor is.

I want you to imagine that getting rich is like a minefield. If you try walking blindly through a minefield, you are going to get blown up, and that's it—game over. Now let's imagine that you are playing a minefield video game, and hitting a mine doesn't kill you, it just makes you start over from the beginning of the game (on the same minefield every time). Each and every time you try to walk through the minefield, you will learn a little bit more about where each mine is, but it will take you hundreds of tries to finally learn enough to walk through the whole thing in one piece.

Competitive friends will give you the motivation to get through the minefield, yes. But only a mentor can get you through the minefield ten times faster and with one-tenth of the effort.

So what is a mentor anyway? A mentor is a person who has already accomplished what you want to accomplish and knows the problems you are going to run into. More importantly, they know the cheat codes to hack your way to the top as fast as possible.

Now, what I want to do for the remainder of this chapter is explain where to look and what to look for in a mentor.

NEVER PURSUE WAYNE GRETZKY

The first lesson in finding a mentor is understanding that you need a suitable mentor. A suitable mentor is someone who is a few steps ahead of you in business, making about ten times what you're making. For example, if you were just beginning to learn how to play hockey, getting a lesson from Wayne Gretzky would be wasted on you. Wayne Gretzky knows how to play hockey at the highest possible level, and because of this, he would probably have trouble understanding (or remembering) the problems of a complete beginner. He would also have to waste weeks teaching you how to skate properly, when his actual expertise is playing hockey. Because of this, only an advanced player could truly benefit from his mentorship. Gretzky would understand the problems of the advanced player because he relates better and probably sees those problems quite often in other people around him.

On the flip side, a beginner hockey coach or a person playing in an amateur league (or even an advanced ice skater) would have a great positive effect on a beginner. Why? Because they understand the exact problems a beginner has and they know how to quickly fix them. This is, again, because they experience or see these problems on a regular basis.

In addition to these facts, getting Wayne Gretzky to coach a beginner would be nearly impossible. Not only would Gretzky probably not want to teach a person how to skate backwards without falling down every ten seconds, but a beginner probably doesn't have the money to pay Gretzky what he's worth when there are thousands of other, more advanced players who would be willing to pay him the money he deserves.

This is common sense, but I see people make this mistake all the time. Every day, I get hundreds (yes, hundreds) of messages online from people who have never built a website asking for mentorship on starting a software company. I want these people to have success, but my time would be wasted teaching someone how to setup a basic website. These people would also probably not want to (or be able to) pay the coaching fees I charge. And lastly, my expertise is in building a software company, so why would I waste my time and energy on helping someone build a website (which is the stuff I make my employees do anyway)?

I've also seen newbies message my friends with net worths of up to $500 million and ask them to teach them how to build a business. The God-honest truth is that my friends couldn't do that even if they wanted to. They are thinking and moving at such high levels that they have no idea how to explain what they do (or did) to a complete beginner.

Because of these facts, you'll want to look for a mentor who is above you, but not too above you. If you are making close to nothing, you want to find someone generating about $3,000 to $5,000 a month in earnings. This type of person will be able to give you the most relevant advice on getting started, because they were in your position pretty recently. They are moving at a level higher than you, but not so high that you can't understand them or they can't understand you.

This is why participating in a large community is so important when you are starting out. You will meet a few people who are doing much better than you but can still relate to you. These people will be able to teach you what to learn, who to learn from, and what to avoid.

In short, if you are a total beginner, find someone playing in the amateur league instead of trying to get mentorship from your niche's Wayne Gretzky.

FINDING REAL MENTORS AND AVOIDING FALSE MENTORS

There is definitely no shortage of people trying to make money in the coaching world, but there are definitely two types of mentors: mentors who make most of their money mentoring and mentors who make money from their main business and just mentor on the side.

What you want to look for is a person whose main business is *not* mentoring. That would be like taking hockey lessons from a hockey fanatic who might know all the rules but has only gotten on the ice a dozen times in his life. There are tons of entrepreneurs making hundreds of thousands of dollars a year that do not coach or mentor. This is because they are busy running their own businesses. These are the people you want to get a mentorship from because they are doing what you want to do, have made the same mistakes you might make, and have taken steps similar to those that you are taking to succeed and become wealthy.

For example, if you are looking to start a business based around selling insurance, you do not want to go and join a giant, $2,000-advertised coaching program lead by some celebrity insurance seller. What you want to do is find someone generating around $5,000 to $10,000 a month whom no one knows about and pay him $1,000 to teach you strategies and give you advice. You can easily find these guys in Facebook groups, forums, events, etc., and talk to as many people as possible. Once you find someone who fits the description of your perfect mentor, ask them if they'd be interested in helping you. Even if they don't have the time to help you, they might be able to give you the contact information of someone who can.

This is a very simple lesson. Again, you want to find someone who is at a level of success you desire to achieve in the near future who was also in your shoes relatively recently (maybe six to twelve months ago).

CHOOSE OTHERS WHO BRING YOU UP RATHER THAN THOSE WHO DRAG YOU DOWN

Trying to become rich without surrounding yourself with other people with the same mind-set is like trying to become good at basketball without knowing any other basketball players. It just doesn't happen that way.

With the right people in your life, you will be driven to be successful and have the cheat codes to get there. It's like the steroid shot of success. On the flip side, if you surround yourself with *only* traffic fighters, you are going to have an extremely hard time escaping your own inner loser. These people will fill you with what-ifs and fears because they know nothing else.

At our core, we humans are merely mimic machines. Our language, our thoughts, our nuisances are all derived from the people we surrounded ourselves with. Yes, at a certain level, we are our own people. But it is undebatable that we are greatly affected by who we look up to and the community with which we surround ourselves. I hope that this chapter really made you think about your current community, and I hope you can find the right balance of mentors, competitive friends, and traffic fighters in your life.

THE SECRET PILLAR
MAKING THE DECISION TO BE WEALTHY AT ANY COST

I want to share with you something that I find terribly sad. Once people start reading a book, they (generally) only read 10 percent of it before they give up or forget about it. Only 10 percent.

What's sad about this is that from this statistic, we can see that very few people actually follow through on what they commit to (at least when it comes to reading). The reason for this is harsh but understandable: most people are too spineless to hold themselves accountable. People "want" and "want" all day, but very few actually have the fortitude to put in the work, even when they know undeniably that this is the best way to achieve success.

Did you know that only 4.4 percent of people who try to lose a large amount of weight (20 percent of their total weight or more) successfully do it and manage to keep it off? This blows my mind. Despite the health risks, social humiliation, and possible low self-esteem that comes with being overweight (because our society still likes to make fun of fat people), a vast majority of people cannot follow through on something as simple as eating less than two thousand calories a day and exercising three times a week.

So what's my point? First, I am trying to tell you that if you are reading these words in the final chapter of this book, you are a statistical anomaly (and I am grateful for you). But here's the kicker: in order to become wealthy as a result of this book, you are going to have be in the .1 percent.

Let's make up a new statistic about books right here on the spot. Imagine that a whopping 20 percent of people who start reading this book actually finish reading it (that sounds about right, I think). I guarantee that only one out of a hundred of that 20 percent will actually become successful because of what they learned in this book. The vast majority of people are going to think, "Yeah, I can do all of this. This is easy. I'll be rich by next summer," but they'll end up taking this information and applying it for a week until they get tired of the hard work and choose to return to their comfort zone.

They are going to *want* to be rich, but they are going to *choose* to stay poor. Getting rich and being successful is a pain in the ass. It's a hell of a lot harder than losing tons of weight, and only 4.4 percent of people (who try) can actually accomplish that. I also say this from experience. I lost close to twenty-five pounds this last summer. I did it by simply eating less crap food, which was far easier than all the work I had to do to become rich.

So, in short, the chances of you becoming successful are slim to none. You have basically just wasted your time reading this book, but I do thank you for the money you donated to me upon purchase to help me become more successful. If we go by statistics, you truthfully are just plain hosed. You'd be better off going back to your traffic fighter life.

Unless you make the decision to be above the statistics.

Look at it this way: every single person in the world has already won the statistics lottery. Did you know that over 100 million sperm are released when people are doing the bow chicka wow wow? For some reason, though, YOU exist, and all your friends and family exist, and billions of strangers exist too. Do you know what that means?

It means that you beat a hundred million other sperm to the punch. Your exact DNA structure and who you are as a human was close to impossible to achieve, but you did it! You are already statistically luckier than a person who has won the lottery six times (the chances are about one in fourteen million).

There are literally a hundred million reasons why you should not be here, alive, on this earth. But you are. There are also a million reasons why you will probably not become rich, but you will become rich if you are determined, dedicated, and never give up . . . just like all those sperm that have turned into human beings. (This is the last time I mention sperm in this book, I promise!) If you decide to follow through no matter what and never give up, becoming rich will not be a matter of *if*, it will be a matter of *when*.

Sure, 96 percent of people can't lose a substantial amount of weight. And sure, most people cannot follow through on anything they set their mind to. But you know what? You are not those other people. Those other people suck. What you need to remember is that everyone has a choice. Wanting it is not enough. You must *choose* to be successful.

Every overweight person had a choice. Every person who is not rich had a choice. There was not some statistic Nazi ninja who fell out of the sky and stopped them from succeeding. There was no statistic policeman that pulled them aside and said, "Look, only 4 percent of people can lose weight this year. We apologize, but we are going to have to force feed you donuts." There is no wealthy Batman who swung around the city and stopped 99 percent of people from becoming rich by sabotaging their business.

Every person who failed at something failed because they chose to fail. There was no statistical dice roll. No outside force. No cop feeding them donuts. They decided to take the easy way out and become part of the statistic.

And hey, some people don't want to lose weight. Some people don't want to be millionaires. And that's fine; I'm not talking about them. I'm talking about the people who want it, the people who may have started working towards a goal but then gave up after a week or six months because it was too difficult, too much work, or because they had some other lame excuse (yes, excuse) to go back to their comfortable lives.

What I am trying to tell you is that if you truly commit to something and work at it, the only person who controls your chance of succeeding is you. People will tell you that you are likely to fail. People will say that you're taking too many risks. People will try to convince you to go back to the life of mediocrity they have chosen because they secretly don't want to watch you succeed. Nothing is more painful than watching someone you think is just like you leave you in the dust and become something greater, because then you have to face the reality that *you* could have done that but chose not to.

Don't listen to unsuccessful people. I repeat, do not listen to unsuccessful people—99 percent of people don't know jack about anything and can't even commit to tying their own shoelaces. (Why do you think Velcro became so popular back in the day? Laziness and commitment issues, that's why. I'm kidding, of course, but you get my point!) My advice is that you listen to your mentors, your competitive friends, and yourself *only*.

What you have been given in this book are lessons and mind-sets that the wealthiest people on earth all share. The only difference is that millionaires and billionaires went through pain and trial and error to learn these mind-sets while all you had to do is read this book. I have adopted these pillars (and decided to write them down in book form) because my personal success and the success of everyone around me proves to me that they are all not only true but necessary. Now there is just one more pillar/mind-set/decision/belief that you must adapt to become wealthy. Ready?

THE ELEVENTH PILLAR: DECIDE TO BECOME WEALTHY

Every self-made wealthy person decided to become rich at some point. They said, "Screw statistics, screw whatever tries to get in my way, and screw logic. I want to be rich, and I will be rich!" In order for this book to have any impact on your life, you have to make this decision and truly believe it with every fiber of your being. You can read this book and mentally jerk off to the idea of being rich as much as you want, but until you decide to "get rich, or die trying," you will not get there.

When you are doubting if you can become rich, or when traffic fighters are trying to keep you in their comfort zone, apply the first pillar. Decide to forget what you have been told about wealth from people without wealth, and decide to believe in what actual wealthy people believe (and what this book teaches you).

When you are building a business and you're not sure if you are creating wealth the right way, you can refer to the second pillar. Simply ask yourself if you are separating your time from money or if you are simply creating another job.

When you are intimidated by a problem that you might not be able to solve, think about the third pillar. Conquer your challenges by accepting the fact that you *must* be greater than any challenge (or person) that comes your way.

When you are moving forward in your business and want to prevent setbacks, go back to the fourth pillar. Remember that you are solely responsible for everything that happens to your business. When you do this, you will be able to predict and fight problems that are outside your assumed responsibility.

If you are letting fear stop you from expanding and taking financial risks, ask yourself if you are adopting the fifth pillar. Try to recognize whether you're thinking with the abundance mind-set of a future billionaire or the scarcity mind-set of an eight-to-five traffic fighter.

When you are deciding what to focus on, but you're not making any progress, think back to the sixth pillar. Pinpoint the immediate problem you have that is stopping your progress, and solve that first. Do not let yourself get distracted by what-ifs. Instead, focus on what is.

If you are falling into the bad habit of setting mental mas-turbation goals, a.k.a. giant goals that have no plan of action to obtain, remember the seventh pillar. Go back and break down your goals into smaller goals, and then break those goals down into even smaller actions that you can do today.

When you are moving forward with your business and thinking about how other people can help you, reread the eighth pillar. It is imperative that you remember that people are going to make you rich, and in order to get rich, you need to convince people (in a good way) to give you money.

If you find yourself struggling to make money, reflect on the ninth pillar. Check to see if you are focusing on low ROI actions and looking past what is actually getting you paid, and then switch your focus solely to high-ROI actions (and make other people do the rest).

The next time you are hanging out with your friends, ask yourself if you are really attempting to live out the tenth pillar. Are you interacting with people that move you forward and drive you to succeed? *Or*, are you hanging out with people that keep you in a traffic fighter mind-set?

Most importantly, before you apply any of these other pillars and attempt to make them a part of your life, you must adopt the one pillar that you can use right now, no matter where you are in your life or your business. This is the eleventh pillar: making the decision to get rich no matter what.

You can make this decision right this second. Not tomorrow, not next week. Not next month or when you have some money saved up. Not when the kids are out of the house, not when you retire, and not when your pesky cold goes away. Right now!

You can adopt the eleventh pillar and decide to live a life of abundance right this second. But you can't just make this decision once and expect to get rich by next Tuesday. You are going to need to adopt this pillar every moment of every day. While you're on your success journey, there will be 1,001 forces trying to make you renege on this promise that you have made to yourself.

Because of this, you must make and recommit to this decision every single day. There are no maybes. There are no I'll-do-it-tomorrows. You must embrace this idea and mindset with every fiber of your being every second of your life. Every decision you make and action you take must line up with your goal of becoming wealthy. This belief must completely consume you.

Once you have adopted this pillar, all you have to do is apply the other ten pillars, and success will be yours, which *is* as simple as I just made it sound. It's not a statistic or chance or luck. You either do it, or you don't.

So, I am going to leave you with one final exercise. In the box on the next page, I want you to write, "I will become wealthy."

Then, below this commitment to yourself, I want you to sign your name and write today's date. This is your promise and commitment to yourself that you will not be a statistic. You won't be like the other people who accept living a mediocre life of scarcity and unfulfilled wants. You are promising yourself that you will live a life of abundances and achieved dreams.

If you cannot make good on this promise to yourself daily, then don't sign it. I don't need you to blame me or this book for your failures. But if you can write that statement and firmly believe it, then go ahead. Do it. Then rip out this signed page and tape, glue, or staple it to a spot where you will see it every single day when you wake up, like on your bathroom mirror, on your coffee maker, or on your spouse's forehead. It is important that you read this statement every morning so that the first thing you think about is this promise that you made to yourself.

(Also, if you have a Twitter or Instagram, you should take a picture and tag me at @AlexBeckerTech with the hashtag #10Pillars. Seriously, do it! This is a powerful exercise, because now you are publically holding yourself accountable as well. Whenever I want to make a big commitment, I announce it publicly so that I cannot go back on it without embarrassing myself.)

MY PROMISE

Name: Date:

It all comes down to this: Make the decision. Make the decision . . . and make the decision. I cannot emphasize this enough. Adopting the mind-sets in this book can make you millions of dollars, but they are useless without the simple decision to actually become rich. There was a moment in every single self-made millionaire's and billionaire's life when they made the decision to become financially free. While the results were not instant, this single decision—this single moment—changed their lives forever.

After you read this book, I want you to listen closely to all the people around you who want to be rich. Listen to them complain about their eight-to-five jobs and want more out of life. Listen to them talk about that business they will start when they find the time. Listen to them worry about simple bills and fret over the price of dinner at a restaurant. These people all want to be financially free and would love to be wealthy. In fact, almost every person you see wants to be rich. That hobo you see under the bridge wants to be rich. Your family members want to be rich. The next person you see after you finish this book wants to be rich. But they have not decided to become rich. They have accepted a life of financial limits and a life of unfulfilled wants.

Everyone experiences the deep desire to become wealthy at least a few times in their lives. However, less than 1 percent of people will decide to become rich at any cost. I want this moment, right now, to be *your* moment. There is no statistic that applies to you. There is nothing too big for you to handle. There is nothing you want that you can't have.

Every wealthy person on the planet has had this moment, whether they wanted more, were fed up with their boss, or just got sick of being poor. *Every* wealthy person has been where you are right now.

The only thing separating you from them is this final pillar. Make the decision right now to truly commit to becoming wealthy. If you are truly committed, no risk will be too daunting. No action will be too tiring. No challenge will be too great.

What makes you different from current millionaires and billionaires is that you have a head start because you read this book and know these pillars/mind-sets before you even start. Reading this book will mitigate your mistakes and lessen the time it takes for you to become successful (if you truly adopt them). So, decide to be wealthy and leave the rest of the world behind. Decide what type of life you are going to live and who you are going to be. Decide that you deserve whatever comes your way, so you might as well make it good.

This is your moment. Make the decision to become wealthy. Right. Now.

STARTING YOUR OWN BUSINESS THE "RIGHT WAY"

Hopefully, by now you have learned (and possibly already have adopted) some new mind-sets that will change your level of success. As I stated in the first chapter, income is the result of our actions, and actions are the results of our beliefs. Therefore, if we want to become rich, the hardest but most necessary challenge is changing our belief system.

In this bonus chapter, I am going to get away from the mind-sets for a minute and give you some tactical advice on how to get started in the business/entrepreneur/wealth world. More so, I want to teach you some tactics that will minimize risk and maximize reward.

(Note: I have also created a completely free business quick start video series at AlexBecker.org/go. Simply go to the URL and you can get the entire course at no charge.)

Please keep in mind that I would have to write half a dozen books to fully explain all of these types of businesses and how to start them. I simply wanted to give you some ideas so you could get the ball rolling right now.

There are thousands of ways to become wealthy. Some people start a business, some people invest in the stock market, and some people go on reality TV shows. No matter what you want to do, as long as you apply these eleven pillars of wealth and never give up, you *will* eventually become rich.

Now, let's talk about how to start your first business.

UNDERSTANDING THE THREE DIFFERENT KINDS OF BUSINESSES

Here's a fun (obvious) fact: not all businesses are the same. And I don't mean some businesses are grocery stores and some businesses are vacuum repair stores. (Do those even still exist?) I mean, the ways businesses start, run, and become profitable are all completely different. Here are the big three:

Cash Flow Businesses (CF)

Cash flow businesses are businesses that have very little overhead but take a lot of personal time to start and run. For example, if you sell online marketing services and do not have a staff, your hard cost is going to be near zero (basically, you just need enough money to buy a domain name and some hosting for your website), but you will be spending a lot of time getting clients and actually providing the service. Because of this, you can bring in a profit at a high margin, usually close to 90 percent.

The issue with this type of business is that everything relies on you. You are the only person selling, marketing, and working, which limits the amount of clients you can have. This means you will eventually and inevitably plateau at some point. Also, these businesses are almost impossible to sell since removing yourself from the equation is nearly impossible. (a.k.a. you cannot separate time from money in this business.)

So, the main benefits of this type of business are:
- High profit margin.
- No investment to start.

And the cons are:
- Time intensive.
- Difficult to scale past a certain point.

Note: Cash flow businesses can transform into High Investment Scalable businesses at a certain point, which I will talk about right now.

High Investment Scalable Businesses (HIS)

High Investment Scalable businesses are the types of businesses you hear about in news stories. They are those apps or massive businesses that explode out of nowhere, making millions of dollars. The core to making these businesses succeed is, of course, building them the right way (hiring the right staff, choosing the right business venture, getting into the right marketplace, etc.). But HIS businesses also cost quite a bit of money to start.

An example of this would be starting a software company. Depending on the type of software you are building, it could require $10,000 to $500,000 to get your first sellable version completed and ready to go. Then, it will cost even more to market the software and start bringing in buyers. The benefit of this, though, is that once the business is set up it can scale to the moon with ease.

When it comes to software, maintaining it at ten users is not much different than maintaining it at a hundred thousand users (unlike a cash flow business). The software will do its job automatically, and the staff you hired to design it will grow in order to maintain it. Because of this, these types of businesses are highly sellable, and it is possible to get nine-figure valuations with a proper setup.

The reason for this is because the business can be operated by anyone since your personal time is not involved. For example, if you have a social media app business that is doing $12 million a year, it would be fairly easy for Facebook to buy you out and integrate it with their current platform (they did this with Instagram, actually).

What's crazy about these types of businesses is that often the creators do not even try to create a profit for years. Amazon is a perfect example. In its first twenty years in business, Amazon did not make a dime, but was worth billions because of how fast it was growing. The reason businesses can do this is because of the perceived potential profit. While they were in reality not making any money, all signs pointed to Amazon becoming the biggest online retailer in the world. Funny enough, Amazon actually outdid every business on the planet in 2015's Black Friday sales, so you can see that this future valuation was well founded. It required an insane amount of money and time to get to that point, though.

So here are the pros of an HIS business:
- Highly sellable.
- Able to be automated.
- Easy to scale into extreme riches.

Here are the cons:
- Expensive to start.
- Cannot usually be done by yourself.
- Can be profit negative for years.

Long-Term Investment Businesses (LTI)

Long-term investment businesses are businesses that take a lot of money to start up but can yield a 10 percent to 20 percent ROI year after year with very little time and very little risk. For example, if you bought a bar that makes $200,000 a year for $1,000,000, you would make a 20 percent return from the business year after year as long as you maintained the business. More times than not, these businesses are brick and mortar businesses that are not going away any time soon and are easy to maintain. For lack of better words, these are businesses at which you can park your money and get a consistently safe ROI.

The best example of this would be real estate. If you bought a ton of apartments and rented them out to dozens of people, you would consistently get an ROI. On top of this, the apartments would hold their value and be sellable for what you bought them for at any time as long as the property value remained the same.

These types of businesses are great investments because they are turnkey and low risk. On the flip side, these businesses require a very large initial investment and are impossible to scale by themselves. For example, you can only make so much money from a single bar location, and scaling it would require you to open a second location, which also has a capped amount of revenue. You will also likely not make your money back until a couple of years after the business opens.

So, here are the pros of an LTI business:

- Safe and consistent investments.
- Easy turnkey and passive income.
- Can generate a high ROI year after year.
- Sellable for the initial value as long as maintained.

And here are the cons:

- Takes a large investment to start.
- Takes a long time to make your money back.
- Almost impossible to scale by themselves.

WHAT DO THESE TERMS AND DEFINITIONS HAVE TO DO WITH ANYTHING?

The reason why you have to know about these three types of businesses is because, if you plan correctly, you can overcome any "con" I mentioned. But if you start off in the wrong business with the wrong idea and mind-set, you will have a huge uphill battle in front of you that might end in unnecessary failure.

Whenever I see new entrepreneurs start an HIS- or LTI-style business, they usually fail *and* lose a ton of money because they have zero experience running a business and have to take a substantial financial risk. This is like removing the safety net while trying to walk a tightrope for the first time in your life. Do people succeed in these situations? Of course . . . but it's rare. Is it the safest way to start a business as a beginner? Definitely not. This doesn't mean you shouldn't chase a dream you truly believe in just because it's an HIS or LTI business; this means that you must plan correctly so you don't make the mistakes most other entrepreneurs make.

HOW TO START A BUSINESS AND MAKE MONEY AS FAST AS POSSIBLE WITH A SMALL BUDGET

If you are reading this book, I am going to assume that spending your life savings to start a business makes you pretty uncomfortable. And if you are just starting out, I will straight-up tell you that you are likely going to fail. Why? Because *everyone* fails. Yes, you have a giant advantage now that you know these insider secrets, but that doesn't mean you will be a billionaire on your first try. It just means that succeeding will be easier and quicker than for the people who haven't read my book. (Cocky? Nope, just confident in my methods.)

My first ventures failed, and there is absolutely no shame in that. But failing does suck pretty badly, especially if you are not prepared for it. So, I am going to show you how to build experience while mitigating risk and making a lot of money at the same time, and this involves starting a cash flow business.

Cash flow businesses are the easiest way to make money right away. Then, if you have bigger goals, you will be able to use your CF profits to fund an HIS business. Then, once you make a lot of money, you can reinvest it into an LTI business that will allow you to sit back and collect an 8 to 15 percent ROI on your invested money year after year if you invest wisely. This will make you passively, outrageously rich (meaning rich without having to work . . . separating time from money).

To put this into perspective, imagine if you sold your company for $15 million. Then you bought one hundred fifty apartments for $100,000 each that all have an annual rent of $15,000 (15 percent annual return). As long as property values remained stable, you would net a 15 percent annual return on your $15 million, which is $2.25 million a year. On top of this, you could liquidate your apartments and get that $15 million back. This is why these LTI businesses work so well—because you can simply park your money somewhere and make a significant return.

Let's go through each business type step-by-step so you can see how to use them together to make tons of moolah.

HOW TO START A CASH FLOW BUSINESS

First and foremost, despite their cons, CF businesses can actually create a large chunk of change by themselves. I have plenty of friends who make $1 million to $10 million a year from cash flow businesses. The problem with this type of business is that they are very time consuming, and you cannot automate them. Therefore, they are nearly impossible to sell. My personal goal is to have a net worth of $100 to $500 million, and that is nearly impossible to reach with a CF business (to make this much, you really need an HIS business, which is what I'll go over next). You might have different goals, so feel free to stop at this step (solely having a CF business) if you want.

Before we start: The best place to start a cash flow business right now is on the Internet (duh). Since the Internet is so vast, it is quite easy to start a business in any niche with a low budget and turn it into a large return business. I want to give you three good places to start looking.

1. AFFILIATE MARKETING

Affiliate marketing is where you sell another person's products and collect a commission. For example, if I own a website where I review guitar strings and then send readers to buy the strings that I suggest using my affiliate link, the guitar string company would send me a commission. Another example would be if I somehow sent traffic to a company's acne product. If people buy the product, the acne company would pay me a commission. All you have to do is sign up for the company's affiliate program before you start selling, and they give you your own special link to use for their product that will track your commission.

This type of business is great because it takes no investment on your part (besides website costs and maybe some ad space). You do not have to create a product or manage its delivery to customers. Your sole job is to send targeted traffic to the product in hopes someone will buy it. You are the epitome of a middleman.

For example, as I've mentioned a few times in this book, one of my first businesses was based around SEO. In short, I was very good at making websites show up at the top of the search engines for relevant searches. So, for example, when people would Google "piano lessons," my website that promoted piano lessons would show up on the first page of Google. Then I would send the traffic to a piano lesson website, which in turn would pay me for every sale I sent to them.

There are 1,001 ways to do affiliate marketing online, though, and focusing on SEO is just one of those ways. Some people buy ads and send people to sellers' websites. Other people buy e-mails and send a seller's offers to people. Others create blogs, Instagram pages, or anything that attracts fans and readers, then promote relevant affiliate products to their followers.

2. Info Marketing

Info marketing is exactly what it sounds like: the selling of information. Go and visit sites like JVZoo.com or ClickBank.com and you will see people making millions of dollars selling products that teach people about any topic under the sun. Dating, getting rid of acne, getting a six-pack, how to make money, how to revive dead plants, it's all there. The reason why I suggest this is because info products:

- Take no money to create.
- Are the easiest types of product to create.
- Can be sold instantly via online download.

On top of this, I am going to assume that you are really, really good at something. Maybe it's knitting or how to stand up to bullies or how to keep goldfish alive for more than a week. Whatever that something is, there are probably other people who want to learn about it. All you really have to do is pick a topic, write a course or eBook explaining all you know about that topic, and sell it on a site like JVZoo or ClickBank.

Info marketing is a topic that I could talk about for days on end, but I can't explain everything that I know in this little chapter. If this seems like something you'd enjoy doing, I'd highly suggest checking out *The Official Get Rich Guide To Info Marketing* by Dan Kennedy.

3. Marketing, Consulting, and Direct-Selling Based Services

Out of the three suggestions for CF businesses, I recommend this one the most often. Why? The above two suggestions require you to learn quite a bit about how the Internet works, and obtaining true wealth from them will take a while. But I consistently see people get rich quickly using this third method based around direct selling. This is because the only thing separating you from a payday is convincing someone to give you a check. Once you get good a convincing/selling to people, you can accumulate large checks very quickly. There is no investment to picking up the phone and selling, and there can be an almost instant reward in doing so.

What is direct selling? It is anything that you can directly sell to people and businesses at a high profit margin. The reason this is so lethal is that the only thing you really have to learn is selling, and it takes zero investment until AFTER you create the sale. A few examples of this would be selling real estate, marketing services (SEO for clients or advertising management), or business consulting.

Let's imagine you decide to pursue selling real estate. Of course, you would have to loosely learn the ins and outs of how to sell real estate, but once you got good at selling it, you could go from $0 to $20,000 a month with zero investment. The same goes with marketing services. I have seen *so* many people learn how to perform SEO or manage people's paid advertising and then generate hundreds of thousands of dollars a year simply by selling the hell out of it. When you are selling something, you can charge $1,000 per month per client, and you won't need that many clients to make $100,000 or more a year.

This is why I have spent many paragraphs in this book pushing you to learn selling above all other things. In most high-end services, you can outsource the work, but you cannot and should not outsource the selling.

I would again highly suggest that you pick up some Dan Kennedy books on direct selling. Not only will you learn how to sell directly to businesses, you will learn how to provide selling services for businesses as well.

BE PREPARED TO FAIL, STRESS OUT, AND GO THROUGH GROWING PAINS

Before we continue, I want to be blunt with you. Creating and growing a cash flow business is going to be a challenge. You are going to mess up and probably fail quite a few times. Fortunately, if a CF business fails, you don't lose much. If you start off with an HIS or LTI business, you will probably fail too, but the difference with these businesses is that there is usually a ton of money on the line. If you fail at a CF business, the only consequences are minor embarrassment and learning some necessary lessons (and maybe losing $100).

What you want to do is get used to running and growing your business when the odds are low, which is why starting with a CF business is perfect. Your CF business is going to teach you what you need to know to grow larger businesses and turn you into a hardened businessperson because you have to be completely self-dependent. After a year or two of constant action, you will be able to sell the hell out of anything.

SHOULD YOU QUIT YOUR JOB TO PURSUE YOUR BUSINESS?

Every single person reading this book has probably thought about this question at least once in the past decade, if not on a monthly or weekly basis. And the answer is: It greatly depends on your life situation. If you have little money in the bank and a family depending on your income, you should be a responsible adult and keep your job while working on your business early in the morning or late at night. If you are single with no kids and you have enough money in the bank to pay all your bills and buy daily steak dinners for six months, then it's a different story. You can quit your job and "coast" for a while, or you can stay at your job and rake in tons of money while working incredibly hard. The point I am trying to make is that throwing away your career or job is not required, and you shouldn't do it if it will cause you excess stress or worry. If you do keep your job and want to start a business as well, it just means you're going to have to work more total hours in a day than someone without a career or job.

For example, remember when I told you that I worked at a marketing agency for a little while? I continued working there while I was building my online businesses and even when I was making a full-time income from my online businesses. There is nothing wrong with having a safety net and being smart with your money. When I had free time at work, I worked on my business. When I got home, I worked on my business. On the weekends, while all my friends partied, I worked on my business.

In fact, I kept my job at this agency until I was making $20,000 a month from my online businesses because I liked to play it safe. After quitting my job, though, I reached $50,000 a month (net) within about two months' time and then over $100,000 a month (net) shortly after.

As you can see, having a job definitely slowed down my progress, yet it did not stop me from starting a business or being successful at that business. On top of that, by keeping a job it gave me a constant stream of money to invest into my business and a safety net that allowed me to take more financial risks.

So, having a job while working on your business will A) slow your progress and B) require you to use all your free time on your business. But it will also A) give you money to invest and B) give you a safety net so you can take financial risks. If you quit your job, you will probably reach your goals faster, *but* you will be more bootstrapped due to not having a replenishing income. You need to figure out your priorities before you make this decision, and make sure you make this decision for yourself and your family; don't make this decision because of someone's uneducated advice. (Actually, never make any decision because of someone's uneducated advice.)

WHAT TO DO WHEN YOU HIT A MONEY PLATEAU (HIS AND LTI BUSINESSES)

With a bit of effort and proper business smarts, most CF businesses can easily be scaled to make $1 to $5 million a year in profit. Once you hit the million-dollar mark, you are going to start running into a lot of plateaus. At this point, you will need to make a choice: stick with your CF business, start an HIS business, or funnel your CF income into an LTI business.

What you need to understand is that there is a difference between being rich now and being wealthy forever. If you want to be wealthy forever in a CF business, you must be okay working at your CF business for the rest of your life (since you can't have other people run it for you and you can't sell it). But you also must be aware that your CF business might not last forever because of changes in consumer demand or changes in your ability to perform the work. So, it's always a good idea to consider other options, such as building your business to an HIS business or investing in an LTI business.

I know plenty of people who make hundreds of thousands of dollars a month from their CF businesses and are completely content to stick with them forever. If that sounds like you, then that's great. You found what you love, and you found what works for you, which is amazing. The only thing I suggest is finding ways to automate your business better or manage clients with less of your own personal time. I also suggest finding ways to charge more money for whatever you are selling because this is the only way to increase your income, since your business is likely still based around your individual time (of which you have a finite amount).

On top of this, I highly encourage you to invest/park this money into an LTI business that allows you to make a 10 to 15 percent ROI year after year . . . but I will go over that in a few pages.

Let's say you want to get really rich. Like disgustingly rich, where you can lose $5 million dollars and barely even notice. The easiest way to do this is by converting your CF business into an HIS business or by starting a separate HIS business.

Converting a CF business into an HIS business can sometimes be easy and sometimes be impossible. For example, one of my first businesses was completely based around me. I was the brand, and people wanted to buy information from me and only me. Because of this, I could not exactly bring in employees to handle the business and create the products. You are going to run into this same problem as well if you are a one-man show with a business focused solely around you.

With an HIS business, our goal is to have a business that runs the same whether we have ten customers or one hundred thousand customers. If we do that correctly, we can then scale this business well past the million-dollar-per-month mark with general ease.

Now, the easiest way to convert a CF business into an HIS business is to find ways to clone yourself. Let's imagine you are selling marketing services. All you need to do is hire a staff that can provide the service you are selling (a.k.a. create an agency). Then, at some point, you need to hire people to sell the services for you as well.

As I stated earlier in this book, no one will be able to sell your business quite like you do, and you will always be the best seller of your products or services. However, if you can clone your tactics to smart people (similar to Jordan Belfort in *The*

Wolf of Wall Street), you can pass your selling to others with great results. I suggest you do this after you have perfected your selling strategy so that it's easier to pass it along to others. Eventually, your time will be spent directing people and focusing solely on finding ways to grow the company. This is the end goal; getting to this point means that you've won.

Examples of this would be a web designer creating a web design company or real estate agent getting staff and creating a firm. See the pattern? Basically, you just need to clone yourself as many times as possible.

Now, let's imagine you can't do this or don't want to do this. Let's say that your CF business was your baby, and you don't want to grow it for some reason. But, after twenty-five years doing the same things every day, you are finally sick of it and want to start a completely new and separate business. This means that it's time to take what you have learned from being a businessperson for twenty-five years and create a separate HIS business from scratch. And yes, even if you choose this option, I still suggest starting a CF business before an HIS business for the main fact that your CF business can completely fund your new HIS business.

When starting an HIS business, I encourage you to think big. Your goal is to have hundreds of thousands of customers, so avoid picking small markets. If you are having trouble thinking of HIS businesses, simply go to your local Walmart, look at your phone, or log onto Facebook. You will see thousands of examples thrown in your face. Look at all the products in the store aisles, all the apps on your phone (or even your phone itself), and all the advertisements on Facebook. Behind each of these, there is a person (usually) collecting millions of dollars from thousands of people without ever being there. Everything is automated.

The thing about these businesses is that they usually cost a bit of money to start. This is because they usually require quite a bit of labor to create. For example, if you were starting a protein

STARTING YOUR OWN BUSINESS THE "RIGHT WAY"

powder business, you would need to pay a company to create the formula and then spend quite a bit to get the initial product made (anywhere up to $50,000, like we spoke about earlier in this book). On top of that, you will need to run ads and get storage to house the product, as well as a hundred other things.

The good thing is that you should be able to fund all of this with your CF business fairly easily. You are already successful, so you do not need this business to make money right away (or even at all, in some cases). The other upside is that once this new business takes off, you can not only make ten times what your CF business made with the same amount of effort but also easily sell the business for five or ten times what it's making you. This is how you can go out and get the $100 million payday that everybody dreams about.

With that being said, you will also be doing something that impacts hundreds of thousands of people, which is pretty dang cool. Who doesn't want to say, "I'm the CEO of PayPal," or, "I created 5-hour Energy"? That's just grade A, neat-o stuff right there if you ask me.

Also remember that these businesses don't need to make you a profit for you to be able to sell them. There are countless businesses that sell for hundreds of millions to billions before they ever make a profit. It's all based on where the business is headed or whose business it disrupts.

INVESTING YOUR CF OR HIS BUSINESS MONEY INTO LTI BUSINESSES

Let's imagine you just sold your company for $100 million. Woo-hoo. What are you going to spend it on. Cars? Houses? Private Jets?

If your answer is "Yes, yes, and yes," then you're an idiot, and here is why. If you spend $100 million on buying a house and a private jet and living "the good life," do you know what happens to the money? It goes away *forever*. The second you spend $500,000 on a car, that money is gone forever. The second you spend $100,000 on a private jet to Europe, that money is gone forever. The only way you can make actual cash from these items is if you sell them. But owning these things is *not* going to make you any more money.

Now, let's imagine that instead of buying a house and a jet, you spend all the money on LTI businesses that net you a 10 percent to 15 percent return year after year. Do you know what happens to the money then? It keeps its value while making you a profit . . . it is just transferred somewhere else. And you can always sell your share for what you paid for it at any time. Do you know what you get in return? Renewable money forever!

For example, one of my friends has a net worth of over $500 million. Instead of blowing all his money on polka-dotted unicorns, he invested it all in LTI businesses. Now my friend passively makes over $50 million a year. He invests 90 percent of that into more LTI businesses and "only" spends $5 million of it on himself. (By the way, unless you are incredibly frivolous or have a very expensive hobby, such as buying mansions or covering every inch of your life in diamond-encrusted wallpaper, it is *very* hard to spend $5 million every year.) So, all my friend has to do is follow this pattern and he'll become a billionaire in ten years.

This is why LTI businesses are so amazing.

I want you to understand that starting an LTI business without ever having a CF business is difficult. Say you wanted to buy a bar for $1 million, but you don't have any CF money to spend, so you raise some money and take out loans to buy it. Since this bar is worth $1 million, you will likely make a profit of $200,000 a year, which means it will take you at least five years to pay off your debt.

However, if you already have $5 million lying around that you made from your CF business, parking it in five bar businesses that make you $1 million a year combined is smart and easy.

BET THE FARM WITHOUT RISKING THE FARM

The outline above is simply my opinion on the smartest way to go about becoming rich for life while mitigating much of the risk. Keep in mind that there are tons of exceptions to these ideas and dozens of other ways to start businesses. In fact, most entrepreneurs don't follow the route I just laid out for you. I've seen many people start their first businesses by raising a ton of money to create an app or start a restaurant. This isn't necessarily wrong, it's just harder than the way I just explained.

What I have seen is that the majority of people who start as CF entrepreneurs stay CF entrepreneurs. Most HIS entrepreneurs stay HIS entrepreneurs. Most LTI entrepreneurs stay LTI entrepreneurs. This, to me, *is* a mistake. HIS entrepreneurs could fund their businesses with CF businesses. CF entrepreneurs could maintain their wealth with LTI businesses. There are multiple ways to make these businesses work together for your gain.

My hope is that you'll keep these concepts in the back of your mind and bring them to the forefront whenever necessary. Remember, your first priority is believing that you can be successful and getting out of your traffic fighter mind-set for good. In order to do this, all that matters is that you take action. You can use the blueprint above, or you can say screw it and try to raise a million bucks for software by having a bake sale. The choice is yours.

ABOUT THE AUTHOR

Alex Becker is a multimillionaire tech entrepreneur who has started multiple online software-based businesses.

He has also helped thousands create their first profitable businesses, all from the comfort of his home in Dallas, Texas.

WANT MORE PRACTICAL BUSINESS TRAINING?

Go To: ALEXBECKER.ORG/GO

All readers of *The 10 Pillars Of Wealth* are eligible to receive a complete video course from Alex Becker. This video course will break down:

- Alex Becker's exact businesses and how he grew them.
- How to get started as a beginner in business without substantial risk.
- Five online businesses that are easy to start and explosively profitable.

FOLLOW ALEX BECKER

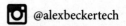 @alexbeckertech   alex becker   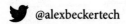 @alexbeckertech

CPSIA information can be obtained
at www.ICGtesting.com
Printed in the USA
LVOW10s2338050218
565454LV00013B/238/P